Osip
Mandelstam's
STONE

THE LOCKERT LIBRARY OF
POETRY IN TRANSLATION
Editorial Adviser, John Frederick Nims

For other titles in the Lockert Library see page 253

Osip
Mandelstam's
STONE

Translated and Introduced by
Robert Tracy

PRINCETON UNIVERSITY PRESS · PRINCETON, NEW JERSEY

CONTENTS

ACKNOWLEDGMENTS

I HAVE CONTRACTED many agreeable debts of gratitude during the preparation of this book. I wish to thank the Chancellor and the Faculty Committee on Research of the University of California, Berkeley for supporting my research and for a sabbatical quarter in which to carry it out. A number of colleagues have been kind enough to read portions of the manuscript: Professor Donald Fanger of Harvard and Professors Joan Grossman, Robert Hughes, Simon Karlinsky, Hugh McLean, and Francis J. Whitfield, all of Berkeley. Professor Gleb Struve patiently answered questions and offered helpful suggestions and clarifications. I am also grateful to Professor Struve for his kind permission to reproduce here the Russian texts of Mandelstam's poems from his own edition of Mandelstam's works. Seamus Heaney made valuable comments on earlier stages of my text.

During the final stages of my work on these poems, I have had the honor and pleasure of serving as the Kathryn W. Davis Professor of Slavic Studies at Wellesley College, where I had an opportunity to test some of my theories in a seminar dealing with Mandelstam and some of his contemporaries. I am grateful to Wellesley for this stimulating opportunity, and I am particularly grateful to Professor Irina Lynch of Wellesley for her careful scrutiny of my text and for many sensitive and helpful comments.

Several of these poems have already appeared in various periodicals: Poem 74 in the *New Orleans Review* 7, no. 1 (1980), Poem 42 in *The Literary Review* 23, no. 3, Spring 1980; and Poems 6, 37, 44, and 78 in *Poetry* 136, no. 1 (April 1980); I thank the editors of these journals for permission to reprint these poems.

My largest debts are to Nicholas Warner, who generously shared with me his own heritage of the Russian language and worked through several versions of the poems to excise tempting inaccuracies; to Joan Trodden Keefe, herself a gifted poet and translator of Irish poetry, who consistently supported this project by scrutinizing, advising, and encouraging; and to my wife, who read and read and read again.

A NOTE ON THE TEXT

MY RUSSIAN TEXT for the translations and for citations from Mandelstam has been the splendid edition of Mandelstam's *Sobranie sochinenii* [Collected works] edited by G. P. Struve and B. A. Filipoff (New York: Inter-Language Literary Associates, 1964-1971); I refer to this in my notes as SS. (The text of Poem 59 is the only exception; it was taken from Dymshitz's and Khardzhiev's *Stikhotvoreniia*, where it appears as Poem 52.) I have used the revised and expanded second (1967) edition of volume 1, which contains most of Mandelstam's poetry; each translated poem appears in the order and with the number assigned to it by Struve and Filipoff, and these numbers are used for all references to poems in my introduction and notes. References to prose passages (all from volume 2) are by volume and page: SS, 2, 137 refers to *Sobranie sochinenii*, vol. 2, p. 137.

In the introduction, titles of works by Mandelstam and other Russian writers are given in English, followed by the transliterated Russian title in parentheses; this procedure is also followed for individual essays and poems referred to in footnotes and in the notes to the poems. However, Russian journals and books cited in footnotes and notes are cited first in transliterated Russian, followed by an English translation of the title in brackets. I have not transliterated titles that are proper names and so are essentially the same in both languages: "Francois Villon," *Mozart and Salieri.*

LIST OF ABBREVIATIONS

The following abbreviations have been used for books and articles cited frequently in the notes.

AAS   Anna Akhmatova, *Sochineniia* [Works], ed. G. P. Struve and B. A. Filipoff (Inter-Language Literary Associates, 1967-1968), 2 vols. Volume 1 was revised and enlarged in 1967, volume 2 in 1968. References are to volume and page: AAS, 2: 169 refers to vol. 2, p. 169.

B   Clarence Brown, *Mandelstam* (Cambridge: Cambridge University Press, 1973).

BP   O. Mandelstam, *Stikhotvoreniia* [Poems], ed. A. L. Dymshitz and N. I. Khardzhiev, Biblioteka poeta [Library of poets] (Leningrad: Sovetskii Pisatel', 1974).

Dante   O. Mandelstam, "Talking about Dante" ("Razgovor o Dante"), trans. Clarence Brown and Robert Hughes, *Delos* 6 (1971). My citations are to this translation. It is reprinted, with some revisions, in Mandelstam's *Selected Essays*, trans. Sidney Monas (Austin: University of Texas Press, 1977). I regret that Professor Monas's fine collection appeared too late for me to make use of it. For the convenience of the reader, I have added page references to the Monas volume and to the Russian text in SS.

Gumilyov   Nikolay Gumilyov, *Sobranie sochinenii* [Collected works], ed. G. P. Struve and B. A. Filipoff (Washington, D.C.: Victor Kamkin, Inc., Book and Magazine Publisher, 1962-1968), 4 vols. References are to volume and page: Gumilyov, 4:171 refers to vol. 4, p. 171.

K1   O. Mandelstam, *Kamen'* (St. Petersburg:

Akmé, 1913). 34 pp. There is a facsimile of this edition published by Ardis Publishers, Ann Arbor, Michigan, 1971. Contents: 8, 14, 9, 13, 24-26, 21, 30, 161, 23, 32, 31, 29, 33, 35, 36, 41, 42, 45, 37-39 (23 poems).

K2   O. Mandelstam, *Kamen'* (Petrograd: Giperborei [Hyperborea], 1916). 86 pp. + 6. Contents: 1-3, 5-9, 12, 11, 13-15, 18-39, 41, 42, 45-47, 40, 48-51, 53-56, 59, 57, 60-64, 67, 68, 71, 69, 72, 74, 75, 77, 78, 80, 81 (67 poems).

K3   O. Mandelstam, *Kamen'*, subtitled "First Book of Poems" ("Pervaia kniga stikhov") (Moscow-Petrograd: Gosizdat [State publishing house], 1923), in the series "Library of Contemporary Russian Literature" ("Biblioteka sovremennoi russkoi literaturi"). 98 pp. Contents: 1, 2, 4-10, 12, 11, 13-15, 18, 20-33, 36-39, 41, 42, 45, 96, 46, 47, 40, 48-55, 59, 76, 87, 57, 60-64, 67, 68, 70, 69, 72-74, 461, 90, 118, 77-79, 66, 65, 80, 81, 460, 136 (76 poems).

K4   Part one of *Stikhotvoreniia* [Poems] (Moscow-Leningrad: Gosizdat, 1928). Contents (of part one): 1, 2, 4-18, 20-33, 36-39, 41-43, 45-47, 40, 48-55, 57-70, 72, 73, 75, 74, 76-78, 80, 81, 82 (74 poems).

P   *The Prose of Osip Mandelstam*, trans. Clarence Brown (Princeton: Princeton University Press, second printing, 1967).

SS   Osip Mandelstam, *Sobranie sochinenii* [Collected works], ed. G. P. Struve and B. A. Filipoff (New York: Inter-Language Literary Associates, 1964-1971), 3 vols. I have used the revised and expanded second edition of volume one (Washington, D.C. and Munich, 1967), which contains Mandelstam's poetry (apart from his translations into Russian), and the first edition of volume two (New York and Munich, 1966). References to prose passages (all from volume 2) are to volume and page: SS, 2:137 refers to *Sobranie sochinenii*, vol. 2, p. 137.

Taranovsky Kiril Taranovsky, *Essays on Mandel'štam*, Harvard Slavic Studies, vol. 6 (Cambridge: Harvard University Press, 1976).

Terras Victor Terras, "Classical Motives in the Poetry of Osip Mandel'štam," *Slavic and East European Journal* 3 (1966): 251-267.

INTRODUCTION

INTRODUCTION
MANDELSTAM: THE POET AS BUILDER

> . . . his multilingual tombstone, like Navellicky Ka-
> men . . .   —Joyce, *Finnegans Wake*

> We stood talking for some time together of Bishop
> Berkeley's ingenious sophistry to prove the non-ex-
> istence of matter, and that everything in the uni-
> verse is merely ideal. I observed, that though we are
> satisfied his doctrine is not true, it is impossible to
> refute it. I never shall forget the alacrity with which
> Johnson answered, striking his foot with mighty
> force against a large stone, till he rebounded from it,
> "I refute it *thus*."
>   —Boswell, *Life of Samuel Johnson, LL.D.*

MANDELSTAM (pronounced Mandelshtám) did not believe
that biographical information about artists was of much
importance. "My memory is inimical to all that is per-
sonal," he declares in *The Sound of Time* (*Shum vremeni*,
1925). "I was never able to understand the Tolstoys and
Aksakovs . . . enamoured of family archives with their
epic domestic memoirs." He defined himself as a *razno-
chinets*, a classless or "upstart" intellectual with no
clearly defined social or official rank, who was committed
to the liberal and human values of the nineteenth-century
Russian intelligentsia. "A *raznochinets* needs no mem-
ory," he explains, "it is enough for him to tell of the
books he has read, and his biography is done."[1] He consid-
ered himself bound to the *raznochintsi* and their values
by an oath "solemn enough to bring tears."[2] During most
of his life, Mandelstam owned nothing but a few books
and some clothing (after the Revolution, when he was
completely destitute, he applied to Gorky through the
Union of Poets for a sweater and a pair of trousers; Gorky
refused the trousers).[3] Only rarely did he have a room of

[1] SS, 2: 137. P, p. 122.
[2] "1 January 1924," SS, poem 140.
[3] Nadezhda Mandelstam, *Hope Abandoned*, trans. Max Hayward
(New York: Athenaeum, 1974), p. 63.

3

his own to live and work in or a desk at which to write—
he usually composed his poems in his mind while walk-
ing the streets and wrote or dictated them only at the end
of the poetic process. "How many sandals did Alighieri
wear out in the course of his poetic work, wandering
about on the goat paths of Italy?" he asked, imagining the
admired Dante sharing his own working habits. "The *In-
ferno* and especially the *Purgatorio* glorify the human
gait, the measure and rhythm of walking."[4] Peripatetic,
homeless, and owning almost nothing long before he was
sent to one of Stalin's concentration camps, Mandelstam
thought of himself as an "internal emigré," an exile in his
own country, and identified himself with the exiled
Dante, with Joseph sold into Egypt (Osip is a form of Jo-
seph), and with Ovid and Pushkin, both exiled to the
shores of the Black Sea by angry emperors.

OSIP EMILEVICH MANDELSTAM was born in January 1891
in Warsaw, then under Russian rule, and died in a transit
camp near Vladivostok, probably at the end of 1938. The
two cities, at extreme ends of the old Russian Empire, are
unlikely locales in Mandelstam's life, for he is identified
with St. Petersburg, the cultural and political capital of
imperial Russia, where he spent his early years. Many of
his poems are about that strange misty city, with its vast
squares, its Roman buildings and Dutch canals. St. Pe-
tersburg's traditional mission was to make Russians
aware of Western European culture, and as a poet Man-
delstam dedicates himself to the same mission by at-
tempting a synthesis of Western and Russian culture, the
latter contained in the Russian language itself.
    The Mandelstams were Jews and, like all Jews in im-
perial Russia, lived in an uneasy relationship to authority
and to their Slavic fellow subjects. The poet's father was
a prosperous leather merchant and a man of standing, al-
lowed to live in St. Petersburg and its suburb of Pavlovsk,
places where Jews were not ordinarily permitted to live.

[4] Dante, p. 68. See also Monas, p. 6; SS, 2:406.

Emil Mandelstam came originally from Riga and spoke German as his first language. Like many nineteenth-century Jews, he had abandoned traditional Jewish ways of living and thinking to become "progressive." His son describes him as enthusiastically exploring, a century late, the startling new ideas of the eighteenth-century Enlightenment.[5]

In *The Sound of Time* ("time rushes backwards with a roar and a swash, like a dammed up stream"),[6] Mandelstam uses the family bookcase as a metaphor for his own intellectual background: on the bottom shelf the "Judaic chaos" of his father's Hebrew books, which the poet could not and would not read; above these the "orderly arrangement" of German books—Schiller, Goethe, Kerner, Shakespeare in German, "my father fighting his way as an autodidact into the German world out of the Talmudic wilds"; and still higher his mother's Russian books—Pushkin, Lermontov, Dostoevsky, Turgenev, the "civic poet" Nadson.[7] Mme. Mandelstam's Russian was "clear and sonorous without the least foreign admixture. . . . Mother loved to speak and took joy in the roots and sounds of her Great Russian speech, impoverished by intellectual clichés." Mandelstam attributes his own preoccupation with words—their value, forms, sounds, their *weight*—to his awareness of the differences in his parents' ways of speaking: "The speech of the father and the speech of the mother—does not our language feed throughout all its long life on the confluence of these two, do they not compose its character?"[8]

The young Mandelstam evaded his parents' half-hearted attempts to have him learn Hebrew and something of his Jewish heritage. He seems to have rejected "the Judaic chaos" for emotional reasons, perhaps even on grounds of decorum. In *The Sound of Time*, he describes his attraction to the pageantry of imperial Petersburg and to the austere order of the city's neoclassic fa-

[5] P, pp. 90-91.
[6] "Pushkin and Scriabin," SS, 2: 356.
[7] P, pp. 81-84.   [8] P, pp. 89-90.

5

cades, "the granite paradise of my sedate strolls."[9] The desire for classical form and spaciousness was to become a central theme in his poetry, along with a hunger for Western culture and a compulsion to become a master of the Russian language, defiantly aware that as a Jew the language was not his birthright. Like Stephen Dedalus, he was at once attracted and excluded by the language of his rulers: "How different are the words *home, Christ, ale, master* on his lips and on mine!" Stephen thinks, talking with an English Jesuit. "I cannot speak or write these words without unrest of spirit. His language, so familiar and so foreign, will always be for me an acquired speech. I have not made or accepted its words."

Nadezhda Mandelstam, the poet's wife, has described Mandelstam's feeling of not "belonging," for him an aspect of being a *raznochinets*. She points out his identification with Parnok, the continually excluded hero of his novel *The Egyptian Stamp* (*Egipetskaia marka*, 1928), and his description of Dante as a *raznochinets* who needs Virgil to be his sponsor and teacher.[10] It has even been suggested that the lines in poem 17

> I grew as a rustling reed
> Where the pond is foul and muddy
> And with languid and tender greed
> Breathe a life forbidden to me

and the image of "cozy mud" in poem 18 express Mandelstam's awareness that he belongs in the "muddy pond" of "Judaic chaos" and not in the light-filled upper air of Russian culture.[11]

[9] P, p. 80.

[10] Nadezhda Mandelstam, *Hope Against Hope*, trans. Max Hayward (New York: Athenaeum, 1976), pp. 175-176.

[11] See Omry Ronen's article on Mandelstam in *Encyclopedia Judaica: Yearbook 1972*, briefly summarized in Taranovsky, pp. 51-54. Taranovsky's third chapter is subtitled "The Jewish Theme in Mandel'štam's Poetry."

When he was nine years old, Mandelstam entered the recently founded Tenishev School, the best and one of the most expensive secondary schools in St. Petersburg. The school was formed on the English model (though as a day school) and provided an education that was liberal in both the educational and the political sense. The curriculum included a thorough grounding in Latin and a very full survey of Russian literature (a whole year was devoted to Pushkin) from its origins to Turgenev and the lyric poet Fet, although Dostoevsky and Tolstoy seem to have been excluded. The school was legally required to limit Jewish students to 5 percent of the student body, but Vladimir Nabokov, a Tenishev student a few years after Mandelstam's time, recalled that 10 to 12 percent of the students were Jews and that the school authorities falsified their reports.[12]

Mandelstam finished at Tenishev School in the spring of 1907, when he was sixteen. He was already writing poetry, and in September we hear of him back at the school to give a reading of his poems. By Christmas of 1907, he was in Paris. He spent most of his time in Western Europe until 1910, living in Paris and paying brief visits to Switzerland and Italy. Though doubts have been expressed about the reality and duration of Mandelstam's Italian visits, the excursions have been confirmed not only by Nadezhda Mandelstam but also by the way in which the experience of Italy and especially of Rome reverberates in Mandelstam's poetry.[13] He also lived in Germany in 1909, where he spent the winter at the university of Heidelberg, attending lectures on Old French literature and on the philosophy of Kant.

[12] Andrew Field, *Nabokov: His Life in Part* (New York: Viking, 1977), pp. 109-127.

[13] N. Mandelstam, *Hope Abandoned*, p. 26. See also Gleb Struve, "Italian Images and Motifs in the Poetry of Osip Mandelstam" ("Ital'ianskie obrazy i motivy v poezii Osipa Mandel'štama"), in *Studi in onore di Ettore Lo Gatto e Giovanni Maver* (Roma: Sansoni Editore, 1962), pp. 601-614. The title has been cited in English as a courtesy to the reader: no English translation exists.

By 1911 Mandelstam was back in St. Petersburg, where he studied philology at the university, but he apparently never took his degree; he was also baptized as a Lutheran, probably to ease his admission to the university, which had a strict Jewish quota.[14] More importantly, he began to publish poems, first in the elegant journal *Apollo* (*Apollon*), one of the most respected magazines of the period, whose name emphasized its dedication to classical principles of decorum. He soon became a frequent contributor to *Apollo* and other journals and began to attend the weekly literary salon at Vyacheslav Ivanov's Petersburg apartment, "The Tower."

A few years later, in the spring of 1913—the year of *Pygmalion, Le Sacre du printemps, A Boy's Will*, the Armory Show, *Alcools, Sons and Lovers, Petersburg, Der Tod in Venedig*, and *Du côté de chez Swann*—Mandelstam published his first book, *Stone* (*Kamen'*), a thirty-six page pamphlet with a pale green cover, containing twenty-three poems. Mandelstam later brought out three enlarged editions of *Stone*: a ninety-two page edition in 1916, a ninety-eight page edition in 1923, and an edition included in his *Collected Poems* (*Stikhotvoreniia*) in 1928. These four redactions of *Stone*, with their shifting contents and arrangement, comprise the book that the reader is now holding. It is the book of a young poet, containing poems written between his seventeenth and his twenty-fifth year, in all the excitement of rapid artistic growth and mastery.

In a sense, I have now told all that the reader needs to know about Mandelstam's biography for a reading of *Stone*. His subsequent publications, adventures, and ordeals are not relevant to this book, and to know about them can lead the reader to search among these poems for foreshadowings of events that are to occur many years later. The two poems about Ovid in exile (60 and 80) seem to prefigure Mandelstam's own eventual fate, con-

[14] B, p. 46. Brown's *Mandelstam* is a valuable and lively book that clarifies the poet's life and work. Those who know Brown's work will recognize the large debt I owe to his researches.

demned, like the Roman poet, for offending his emperor by "*carmen et error*"—a poem and a mistake;[15] and the hope expressed at the end of "Notre Dame" (39), that "From cruel weight, I too will someday make beauty rise," gains an added poignancy. These poems should rather be read as triumphs of form over emptiness ("games that time plays with space," in Beckett's phrase), triumphs of the word over silence, the work of a young poet entering into his "demesne" with astonishing assurance.

MANDELSTAM AFTER *Stone*

If we consider *Stone* as a single book, Mandelstam published only two other collections of poetry: *Tristia* (1922; second edition 1923), whose title, though not of Mandelstam's choosing, further emphasizes his identification with Ovid; and the previously mentioned *Poems* of 1928, which contained three sections: *Stone, Tristia,* and poems of 1921 to 1925. There are also four little books of children's verse, published in 1925 and 1926; the autobiographical *The Sound of Time*; his short novel, *The Egyptian Stamp*; and a collection of essays about poetry entitled *On Poetry* (*O poezii,* 1928).

The period between the first and fourth publication of *Stone* was a time of upheaval and change in Russia: World War I, the revolutions of 1917, the long agony of civil war (1918-1920), the death of Lenin (1924), and the gradual tightening of Soviet control in all areas of life, including literature, occurred between 1913 and 1928. Like thousands of other Russians, Mandelstam spent much of this period as a refugee. He had been exempted from military service and so did not fight in the war but rather spent parts of 1915, 1916, and 1918 in the Crimea, the part of Russia he loved for its sun, warmth, and wine and be-

[15] Ovid *Tristia* 2. 207. Numbers appearing in parentheses following quoted material or titles refer to the poems in the text and will be indicated this way throughout the introduction.

cause he saw it as an outpost of the ancient classical world, the home of Medea and the Golden Fleece. We find him in St. Petersburg when the Soviets seized power in 1917, and later in Kiev, where he met and married—unofficially—Nadezhda Yakovlevna Khazina in 1919 and survived the expulsion of the Soviets and the capture of the city by a vindictive White army. Later Mandelstam left Nadezhda Yakovlevna in Kiev and returned to the Crimea, still untouched by revolutionary disorder: he epitomizes the time and place in his memoir of the period (attached to *The Sound of Time*) by describing the harbormaster's office in Feodosia, where crisp white uniforms, nautical charts, and gleaming clocks and sextants still represented an order that had vanished forever. For a time he was in Georgia, and then made his way back to St. Petersburg—where Gorky denied him the pair of trousers. He and Nadezhda Yakovlevna were reunited in 1921 and legally married in 1922, in the course of further wanderings across Russia. They settled in Moscow for a year, and then received one of the apartments set aside for writers in the former imperial palaces at Tsarskoe Selo, the "imperial village" near St. Petersburg. Mandelstam was beginning to suffer from heart trouble and Nadezhda Yakovlevna from tuberculosis, conditions probably aggravated by the privations of their vagabond years.

Mandelstam suffered from a kind of writers' block between 1925 and 1930 and was unable to write poetry. He had already discovered that many journals were unwilling to publish his work, presumably because of his traditional humanist values and his failure to celebrate the new Soviet regime with conspicuously patriotic verse. He supported himself by writing children's books, by translating novels by Upton Sinclair, Jules Romains, Charles de Coster, and other Western writers, by revising a translation of the novels of Sir Walter Scott, and by occasional journalism. In 1923 he interviewed the young Ho Chi Minh, and characteristically commented on Ho's uneasy relationship with the language of his rulers: "He speaks French, the language of the oppressors, but the French words sound dim and faint, like the muffled bell of his native language."[16]

Mandelstam had one powerful protector, Nikolay Bukharin, a member of the Politburo and head of the Comintern. Bukharin arranged for the publication of *Poems* in 1928 and probably for the publication of *The Egyptian Stamp* and *On Poetry* in the same year; he also arranged an eight-month visit to Armenia for the Mandelstams in 1930,[17] where Mandelstam found that he was once again able to write poetry. But Bukharin's influence was on the wane: he was deprived of all his positions and expelled from the Party by Stalin in 1929, briefly readmitted to favor in 1934, and finally arrested and executed in 1938.

"Constant searching for some shelter, unsatisfied hunger for thought," Mandelstam wrote on his fortieth birthday (1931), summing up the conditions of his life. The search for shelter was met by the contemptuous assignment of three small rooms in the Moscow Writers' Union, the hunger for thought by his reading of Dante and by increasing creative activity. In 1933, Mandelstam's article "Journey to Armenia" ("Puteshestvie v Armeniiu") appeared, his last publication in his lifetime, and was harshly criticized for failing to celebrate Soviet achievements; in the same year he finally obtained a small Moscow apartment.

Mandelstam was arrested in May 1934, apparently because he composed a poem about Stalin and recited it to several friends, one of whom reported the incident to the authorities (the informer was himself soon arrested and died in a concentration camp before Mandelstam did). The poem describes Stalin's complete domination of Russia by emphasizing the weight and reality of the dictator's words—more real than those of other men because they are instantly translated into action. It also jibes at Stalin's

[16] B, pp. 108-109. Brown translates the entire interview. The Russian text is in SS, 2: 246-249.

[17] N. Mandelstam, *Hope Against Hope*, p. 113.

Georgian background by calling him a mountaineer and an Ossetian:

We live, but we do not feel the land beneath us;
Ten steps away and our words cannot be heard,

And when there are just enough people for half a
   dialogue—
Then they remember the Kremlin mountaineer.

His fat fingers are slimy, like slugs,
And his words are absolute, like grocers' weights.

His cockroach whiskers are laughing,
And his boot-tops shine.

He has a rabble of skinny-necked leaders around him,
He plays games with the aid of those who are only half
   human,

Who twitter, who mew, who whimper.
He alone bangs and thrusts.

Decree after decree, he hammers them out like
   horseshoes—
One in the groin for him, in the forehead for him, for
   him one over the eyes, one in the eyes for him.

When he has an execution, it's a special treat
And the Ossetian chest swells.

                              (SS, poem 286; November 1933)

Mandelstam's papers, including all his unpublished poems, were confiscated during his arrest, and he was sentenced to hard labor on the White Sea Canal, a sentence that few survived. Bukharin intervened, and the sentence was commuted to exile in Cherdyn, a small town on the eastern side of the Urals; later Mandelstam was allowed to serve out his exile in Voronezh, a larger and more attractive city. Nadezhda Mandelstam describes their departure for Cherdyn as a departure from

"Europe," the metaphor stressing her sense of physical and psychic dislocation: "I say 'Europe' advisedly," she writes, "because in the 'new' state I had entered there was nothing of the European complex of thought, feelings and ideas by which I had lived hitherto."[18] Mandelstam had a breakdown and tried to commit suicide in Cherdyn; he recovered in Voronezh and, despite his precarious legal position and his inability to earn any money by writing, he enjoyed another splendid period of creativity.

When his sentence expired in 1937, Mandelstam had to leave Voronezh, and found himself not only homeless but destitute as well. He was rearrested in May 1938, sentenced to five years hard labor, and sent to a transit camp near Vladivostok; an official death certificate (unusual for prisoners), issued in 1940, says that he died there of "heart failure" on 27 December 1938. He was formally "rehabilitated" in 1956, but his poems were not allowed to appear in the Soviet Union until 1974, and then only in an edition intended primarily for sale abroad.

The survival of about two hundred poems that Mandelstam wrote after 1930, the poet's own survival after his 1934 arrest, and virtually all of our information about his later life are due to the extraordinary woman who joined her fortunes with his in 1919. Nadezhda Mandelstam managed to avoid arrest during the Stalin era, and later she wrote a remarkable account of her life that is itself a classic of modern Russian literature, although it remains unpublished in her own country. Entitled *Vospominaniia* (1970) and *Vtoraia kniga* (1972), this work has been published in English as *Hope Against Hope* (1970) and *Hope Abandoned* (1974). Her books celebrate and exemplify the traditions of human decency and the preservation of European culture for which the best of the *raznochintsi* stood. She also preserved Mandelstam's poems, concealing manuscripts and copies and even memorizing them in case all copies should be destroyed.

18 N. Mandelstam, *Hope Against Hope*, pp. 113; 41-42.

The beginning of Mandelstam's literary career coincided with an intense period of cultural excitement and achievement in Russia, paralleling the period's political agitation. Russian cultural historians describe the years between 1895 and 1915 as "the Silver Age"—silver only because the epithet "Golden" has already been reserved, by general consent, for the age of Pushkin. The literary scene was dominated by the Symbolists: Alexandr Blok, Konstantin Balmont, Andrey Bely, Valery Bryusov, Vyacheslav Ivanov. Mandelstam's earliest poems are Symbolist in style and feeling, and for a time he considered Bryusov and Ivanov as his mentors: it was at one of Ivanov's "Tower" gatherings that he met two younger poets with whom his literary career was to be closely connected, Anna Akhmatova and her husband, Nikolay Gumilyov; the trio would soon become known as the Acmeist school.

Poets of the period tended to think of themselves as members of groups or schools. Along with the reigning Symbolists, there were the Futurists, led by Mayakovsky and Khlebnikov, while Esenin was the best known among the "peasant" poets. Groups divided and subdivided as frequently as the new political parties in the Duma— there were also the Ego-Futurists, the Imaginists, and the Argonauts.

The other arts were in an equally lively state. Chagall and Vrubel were emerging as painters, Scriabin, Rachmaninov, and the young Stravinsky were revolutionizing music, Stanislavski and Meyerhold were developing new methods in theatrical production, and Diaghilev was reforming classical Russian ballet, while Lev Bakst and Alexandr Benois were everywhere, painting, illustrating books, designing costumes and scenery for ballet and theater. There was a remarkable intensity about it all, as if the participants foresaw that this creativity was soon to be stifled by the Soviets or scattered into foreign exile.

The great achievements of Russian novelists in the age

of Tolstoy, Dostoevsky, and Turgenev had not been matched by the Russian poets who were their contemporaries. Most of them wrote "civic" poetry in a style that Mandelstam described as an "almost wooden simplicity."[19] Their chief concern was to make the reader a better and more enlightened citizen in a gently liberal way. A subjective poet or a poet preoccupied with technique rather than with civic virtue seemed to them a kind of renegade: Afanasy Fet chose to avoid such criticism by publishing nothing for twenty years (1863-1883). The intolerance of the civic poets and critics, and their insistence that the chief purpose of literature is to assist in the forming of the good citizen, reemerged in the 1920s as Socialist Realism, since imposed upon all Soviet writers.

In the 1890s, the Symbolists challenged the prevalent civic theories and succeeded in freeing Russian poetry from what Gumilyov called its "narrow prison of ideology and prejudice."[20] The Symbolists wrote subjective poetry and insisted that poets must be concerned about technique—good intentions were no longer sufficient. A number of first-rate poets appeared to put these principles into action: Bryusov, Balmont, Zinaida Gippius, Sologub, and a little later the second Symbolist generation of Blok, Bely, and Ivanov. At the same time, the Symbolists taught the public how to read both the new poetry and the poetry of the past. The Symbolists also influenced painting, music, and other arts, and they brought Russia into touch with a literary movement that was European rather than national, represented elsewhere by Baudelaire, Mallarmé, Valéry, Maeterlinck, D'Annunzio, Stefan George, Rilke, and Yeats.

By about 1906, the Symbolists had become the literary establishment in Russia and were ready for schism. The younger Symbolists, Bely, Ivanov, and to some extent Blok, came to think of poetry as essentially religious, mystical, and metaphysical. The poet was seer rather

[19] P, p. 83.
[20] Quoted in Simon Karlinsky, *Marina Cvetaeva: Her Life and Art* (Berkeley and Los Angeles: University of California Press, 1966), p. 2.

than craftsman, and he was to seek and record visions of eternal metaphysical truth rather than to concern himself with artistic form. There was also a partial shift of interest away from Western European culture to the Russian or even the Byzantine cultural past: the mystic Symbolists called one of their new journals *The Golden Fleece* (*Zolotoe runo*) to remind people that the Fleece was found in Russia, not by journeying abroad. Valery Bryusov spoke for the older Symbolist values, arguing that poetry was an end in itself and that the poet's chief task was to perfect his technique: "Poets may be evaluated by the worth and the flaws in their poetry, and by nothing else," least of all by "how they communicate with 'The Woman Clothed with the Sun' " or by how they try to write their own book of Revelation.[21] Bryusov cited with approval Gautier's definition of the poet as first of all a worker—a builder, a craftsman[22]—an idea that became the basis of Mandelstam's position and is often echoed in his poetry.

Both the Symbolist split and Bryusov's theory of the poet as craftsman brought two new groups into being, each concerned with poetic technique and each emphasizing certain aspects of Bryusov's teachings: the Futurists and the Acmeists. Each is defined primarily by its attitude toward the basic unit of poetic activity: the word. Futurists and Acmeists agreed that the mystic Symbolists misused words because they were often not interested in a word's objective meaning but only in what it could be made to mean; they were not interested in the real object that a word signified but only in finding a way to make that object a symbol for something else, for some abstract concept—what Mandelstam called "the frightful *contredanse* of 'correspondences,' one bobbing to another." To

[21] Valery Bryusov, "A Defence against Certain Praising" ("V zashchitu ot odnoi pokhvaly"), in *Vesy* [The scales], May 1905, p. 38. The "woman clothed with the sun" appears in Rev. 12:1. See also Martin P. Rice, *Valery Briusov and the Rise of Russian Symbolism* (Ann Arbor: Ardis, 1975), p. 85.

[22] Bryusov, "The Holy Sacrifice" ("Sviashchennaia zhertva"), in *Vesy*, January 1905, p. 25. See also Rice, *Valery Briusov*, pp. 78-85.

the Symbolist, he declared, "a rose, the sun, a dove, a girl ... not one ... is interesting in its own right, but the rose is an image for the sun, the sun is an image for the rose, the dove is an image for the girl, the girl is an image for the dove. They disembowel the original object like a bird about to be stuffed, and stuff it with foreign matter. Instead of a forest of symbols, a taxidermy studio." And he quoted with approval the Acmeist slogan: "Down with Symbolism, long live the living rose!"[23]

Although the Futurists were also opposed to using words as symbols, they were not really interested in a word's lexical meaning. Their concern was with the *form* and sound of a word itself, and Velimir Khlebnikov soon developed his "trans-sense" or metalogic (*zaumny*), treating words as incantations and often exploding them into their roots and derivatives, as in his famous poem "Incantation by Laughter" ("Zaklyatie smekhom," 1910), made up of words derived from the Russian word for laughter (*smekh*):

O rassmeytes smekhachi!
O zasmeytes smekhachi!
Chto smeyutsya smekhami, chto smeyanstvuyut
    smeyalno
O zasmeytes usmeyalno.

O laugh it up you laughletes!
O laugh it out you laughletes!
That laugh with laughs, that laugherize
    laughingly
O laugh it out so laughily
O of laughing at laughilies—
    the laugh of laughish laugherators . . .

Khlebnikov described himself as looking for "a touchstone for the transformation of all Slavic words one into another, for the free fusion of all Slavic words. Such is the

[23] "Concerning the Nature of the Word" ("O prirode slova"), SS, 2: 296-299.

self-valuing word without relation to life or use."[24] Mayakovsky declared that his method was "common sense," but he too was interested in the word in a new way. He used startling, sometimes bizarre rhymes, and made the word his basic unit, often isolating each word or brief phrase in a line of its own until a poem resembles a flight of steps. The Futurists further proclaimed that all the literature and culture of the past ought to be jettisoned "from the steamship of modernity" as useless rubbish and replaced by something completely new.

The Acmeists, the group with which Mandelstam is identified, had different ideas. The Symbolist Bely offered them their name in derision, but they seized it proudly, explaining that in Greek *akmé* meant "the highest degree of something . . . a time of flowering."[25] They had originally come together as "The Poets' Workshop" (*Tsekh poetov*), a name that affirmed their sense of themselves as primarily craftsmen. Gumilyov founded the Workshop in November 1911, with himself and Sergey Gorodetsky as "Masters of the Guild" and Anna Akhmatova as "Secretary"; Mandelstam soon became, in Akhmatova's phrase, "first violin."[26]

In January 1913, Gumilyov and Gorodetsky published Acmeist manifestoes in *Apollo*; Mandelstam also wrote a manifesto, "The Morning of Acmeism" ("Utro akmeizma"), which was not published until 1919. Gumilyov's manifesto, "The Legacy of Symbolism and Acmeism" ("Nasledie simvolizma i akmeizm"), acknowledged the Acmeists' Symbolist ancestry ("Symbolism has been a worthy father"), and claimed that the

[24] Both the poem and the prose passage are quoted from Roman Jakobson, *Noveyshaya russkaya poeziya* [Modern russian poetry] (Prague: Politika, 1921), as excerpted and translated in Edward J. Brown, *Major Soviet Writers* (London: Oxford University Press, 1973), pp. 74-75, 81.

[25] "The Legacy of Symbolism and Acmeism" ("Nasledie simvolizma i akmeizm"), Gumilyov, 4: 171. The essay originally appeared in *Apollon*, no. 1 (January 1913), pp. 42-45. For Bely's and Ivanov's role in naming Acmeism, see B, pp. 139, 305-306.

[26] "Mandelstam," AAS, 2: 169.

Acmeists were the true heirs of Symbolism, preserving the best of the older movement, its tradition of craftsmanship, while abjuring the heresies of writing too subjectively and of making poetry into a handmaiden of mysticism. "It is harder to be an Acmeist than to be a Symbolist," he declared, "as it is harder to build a cathedral than to build a tower"—a dig at Ivanov and the "Tower" mystics. Gumilyov demanded that subject and object be equally important in a poem; that a word's meaning remain fixed, so that it would not vanish into a protean chain of metaphors; and that the poet respect the integrity of each word or phenomenon in itself, which would ensure a respect for each word's value in the scheme of the poem and each phenomenon's value in the general scheme of things. He also called for less rigid metrical forms, and proclaimed Shakespeare, Rabelais, Villon, and Gautier (whose *Émaux et camées* he had translated) as the four cornerstones of Acmeism.[27]

As these names suggest, the Acmeists shared that commitment to Western European culture traditionally associated with St. Petersburg (Bely, Blok, and Ivanov were proclaiming their preference for the traditionally Russian, the Byzantine, the Scythian) and emphasized in the title of the journal *Apollo*, with its classical and orderly implications (Ivanov, in contrast, was attracted by Dionysus). When the Acmeists started their own journal late in 1912, they called it *The Hyperborean* (*Giperborei*): even though they lived in the distant north, the Hyperboreans, according to Herodotus and Pindar, were worshippers of Apollo and considered themselves part of the Hellenic world.[28] Years later, when Mandelstam was pressed to define Acmeism by a hostile audience, he defined it as "a yearning for world culture."[29]

It is customary to describe Acmeism as if it were a well-organized movement with a clearly defined body of doc-

[27] "The Legacy of Symbolism and Acmeism," Gumilyov, 4: 171-178, esp. pp. 172-173.

[28] Herodotus *Histories* 4. Pindar *Pythian Odes* 10. 29-49.

[29] "Mandelstam," AAS, 2: 185.

trine. Some of the Acmeist poets, including Mandelstam, did try to define a set of literary theories that the group held in common, but in fact Acmeism was less a school or movement than it was a quest for greater clarity and precision in poetry. To read the poems of the three best Acmeists is to see this quest for precision at work, but the reader also notices diversities rather than similarities. Gumilyov wanted poetry to be "manly"; consequently he celebrated bravery and stoicism. His poem "My Readers" ("Moi chitateli") describes his ideal audience:

> . . . A man who shot an imperial ambassador
> Amid a throng of people
> Came to shake my hand
> To thank me for my poems.
>
> There are many of these, strong, wicked,
>   cheerful,
> Who have killed elephants and men,
> Who have died of thirst in the desert,
> Frozen on the rim of the eternal ice,
> Who are loyal to our strong,
> Our cheerful, our wicked planet,
> Who carry my books in their saddle bag,
> Read them in a palm grove,
> Leave them behind on a sinking ship,
>
> ....
>
> . . . when bullets whistle around,
> When waves split the ship's side,
> I teach them to be unafraid . . .[30]

1921

[30] Gumilyov, 2: 61. The poem first appeared in Gumilyov's collection *Ognenny stolp* [A pillar of fire, 1921], containing poems written between 1918 and 1921. Gumilyov won the George Cross, Russia's highest award for bravery, during World War I. When he gave the destitute Mandelstam an extra pair of trousers, Mandelstam claimed that he felt "unusually strong and manly" while wearing them. See N. Mandelstam, *Hope Abandoned*, p. 64.

Akhmatova's poems of that period were sparse epiphanies, representing such events as a woman recalling a few concrete details about the ending of a love affair:

> She wrung her hands beneath her dark veil . . .
> "Why are you pale today?"
> —Because I have made him drunk
> With bitter sorrow.
>
> How will I forget it? He went out shaking,
> His mouth twisted with pain . . .
> I ran down, not touching the railing,
> And ran after him to the gate.
>
> Panting, I cried, "It was just a joke,
> That's all. If you go, I die."
> With a calm and terrible smile
> He said, "Don't stand in the wind."[31]
>
> 1911, Kiev

Mandelstam wrote a poetry that is both more impersonal and more allusive. It is concrete but extremely associative: his ideal reader has been trained in "a school of the most rapid associations" to "grasp things on the wing," to be "sensitive to allusions."[32]

All three Acmeists agreed on the importance of precise language and clarity, and rejected mystical experience, considering the real world the only appropriate subject matter for poetry: "That which cannot be known," Gumilyov remarked crisply, "cannot be understood."[33] They were sparing with adjectives, and, while they often wrote subjectively, the "I" of a poem was always placed in the presence of a clearly defined objective reality. The following passages are from three poems with similar set-

[31] AAS, 1: 64-65.
[32] Dante, p. 68. See also Monas, p. 7; SS, 2: 406.
[33] "The Legacy of Symbolism and Acmeism," Gumilyov, 4: 174.

21

tings, by the Symbolist Alexandr Blok, by Akhmatova, and by Mandelstam:

I shall never forget it (did it really happen or not
This evening): the fires of sunset
Burned and drove back the pale sky,
And the streetlights showed against the yellow sunset.

I sat at a window in the overcrowded room.
Somewhere violins sang about love . . .
> Blok, "In the Restaurant" ("V restorane")
> (19 April 1910)

Music jangled away in the garden
With inexpressible sadness.
On a plate, oysters bedded in ice
With a sharp fresh tang of sea.

He said to me, "I am a true friend!"
And touched my dress . . .
> Akhmatova, "In the Evening"
> ("Vecherom") (March 1913)

But I love to be out on the dunes at the casino,
The wide views that the murky window shows,
And thin on the crumpled tablecloth the light;

Green water all around on every side;
When wine shows red in the crystal, like a
    rose—
I love to follow a seagull soaring in flight.
> Mandelstam, "The Casino" ("Kazino," 33)
> (1912)

Blok undercuts his own poem by suggesting the unreliability of the narrator at the very beginning—he is unsure about the reality of his experience and may well be telling us about a hallucination. Akhmatova is quite sure about the reality of her episode: there is no doubt about the oysters on the dish or about the man and the woman's awareness of his physical presence, and the music is not a cliché of romantic violins but real music, and not very well-played at that. The speaker is present as an accurate recorder of her surroundings and her feelings about them. Mandelstam is equally accurate but perhaps a little more impersonal. He is alone with the objects in the casino—tablecloths, wine glass, the green water and seagull outside—and the poem is about these objects rather than about the poet's reaction to them or about the objects as part of the scenery for an emotional encounter.[34] Mandelstam's poem offers a parallel reality in words.

Clarence Brown and other critics have pointed out strong resemblances between Gumilyov's and Mandelstam's theories about the word in poetry and the theories that Ezra Pound was proclaiming as "Imagism" at about the same time, theories that Pound later described as "the revolution of the word."[35] Pound called for clarity and precision not only as technically desirable but as a moral imperative for the poet. "Honesty of the word does not permit dishonesty of the matter," he wrote many years later. "An artist's technique is the test of his personal validity. Honesty of the word is the writer's first aim."[36] For Mandelstam, the central tenet of Acmeism was respect "for the word as such."[37] He shared Gumilyov's respect

[34] For Blok's poem, see his *Sobranie sochinenii* [Collected works] (Moscow-Leningrad: Gosudarstvennoe izdatel'stvo khudozhestvennii literaturi, 1960), 3: 25; for Akhmatova's, see AAS, 1: 99. The translations are my own. The comparison of the poems by Blok and Akhmatova draws on V. M. Zhirmunsky, "Two Tendencies of Contemporary Lyric Poetry" (1920; "Dva napravleniia sovremennoi poezii"), trans. John Glad, in *The Silver Age of Russian Culture*, ed. Carl Proffer and Ellendea Proffer (Ann Arbor: Ardis, n.d.), pp. 60-65. The Russian text is available in Zhirmunsky's *Voprosi teorii literaturi* [Problems of literary theory] (1928; facsimile ed., 'S-Gravenhage: Mouton and Co., 1962), pp. 182-189. Zhirmunsky does not discuss Mandelstam in this article.

[35] Ezra Pound, *Polite Essays* (Norfolk, Connecticut: New Directions, 1937), p. 49.

[36] Pound, *Polite Essays*, p. 193.

[37] "The Morning of Acmeism" ("Utro akmeizma"), SS, 2: 363.

for the word as a phenomenon existing in its own right, but he went further, considering the word in some degree independent even of that which it signifies. In Poem 75, he celebrates the *Imyabozhtsi* or *Imyaslavtsi*, the members of the "God's Name" movement who taught that the name of God is itself divine. For Mandelstam, words are things. They exist in and of themselves and speak for themselves. The poet's task is to find the right ones—the precisely right ones—and arrange them; Eliot makes the same point in "Little Gidding":

> And every phrase
> And sentence that is right (where every word is
>   at home,
> Taking its place to support the others,
> The word neither diffident not ostentatious,
> An easy commerce of the old with the new,
> The common word exact without vulgarity,
> The formal word precise but not pedantic,
> The complete consort dancing together) . . .

For Mandelstam the word does not exclusively or primarily represent an object or concept. "Words are perhaps the hardest of all material of art," Eliot wrote, "for they must be used to express both visual beauty and beauty of sound, as well as communicating a grammatical statement."[38] Mandelstam seems to have looked on each word as "fossil poetry"—Emerson's striking phrase in "The Poet"—and expected it to evoke rather than represent that which it signifies, so that in a poem a word and its significance exist separately but together, like body and soul. In a poem from *Tristia* which begins "We shall gather once more in Petersburg" (SS, poem 118), Mandelstam dreams of pronouncing "the blessed word *without*

[38] T. S. Eliot, *Ezra Pound: His Metric and Poetry* (New York: Alfred A. Knopf, 1917), p. 14. Nadezhda Mandelstam interestingly compares Mandelstam and Eliot in terms of their commitment to the word in *Mozart and Salieri*, trans. Robert A. McLean (Ann Arbor: Ardis, 1973), pp. 43-45.

meaning" (italics mine), and in "The Word and Culture" ("Slovo i kultura"), he asks, "Why identify the word with a material thing, with grass, with the phenomenon it signifies?"

> Is the material thing really the master of the word? The word is Psyche, soul. The living word does not signify a phenomenon, but freely chooses, as it were, one or another objective significance, or concreteness, or cherished body, for its dwelling place. And then the word freely envelops the material thing, as a soul hovers around a body that it has discarded but not forgotten.[39]

In "Concerning the Nature of the Word" ("O prirode slova"), he calls for "the living poetry of the word-phenomenon" or "word-material object."[40] "I do believe,/" Byron had written a century before, "Though I have found them not, that there may be/Words which are things . . ." (*Childe Harold's Pilgrimage*, 3. 114. 1,059-1,061).

Mandelstam maintains the autonomy and preeminence of "the word as such" in his poetry, and avoids subordinating it to ideas or even to its lexical meaning by placing conventional signposts at intervals throughout a poem without letting them point out a real road through the poem. He uses words like *so, therefore, and yet, let us then, but, what then* to give the poem an apparent logical structure behind which the real action—the dance of the "word object"—can go on.[41] Mandelstam is an intellectual poet, but he is not an ideological poet in the way that, say, Eliot and Auden are—he considered it a misuse of poetry to make it serve as argument. In a sense, these are poems about *not* making words convey ideas.

[39] SS, 2: 268. See also B, p. 235.
[40] SS, 2: 301.
[41] I am summarizing Boris Bukhshtab, "The Poetry of Mandelstam," trans. Clarence Brown, *Russian Literature Triquarterly* 1 (1971): 262-282. This is the first appearance of this 1929 essay in print, in any language.

Mandelstam created his own poetic theory and practice out of the cluster of ideas that made up Acmeism, and it is these that govern *Stone*, although in fact many of the earlier poems in the volume are Symbolist poems, as Gumilyov pointed out when he reviewed it (he considered Poem 31, "No, not the moon . . . ," to be the first of the Acmeist poems).[42] *Stone* actually records Mandelstam's development from Symbolism to Acmeism and so records "the growth of a poet's mind," although it hardly seems a prelude since he was a mature poet from the beginning. He himself spoke of the 1913 *Stone*, in the copy he inscribed for Akhmatova, as "flashes of consciousness in the oblivion of days."[43]

Stone Songs

The title *Stone* proclaims Mandelstam's poetic principles. Gumilyov had approvingly quoted Gautier: "Creation is the more perfect/The more passionless the material is!/Be it verse, marble, metal . . . "[44] Among minor Symbolists, titles like *Beryl* or *Chrysophrase* were popular, and even Gumilyov had published *Pearls* (*Zhemchuga*, 1910); Mandelstam's working title for *Stone* before publication was "Seashell" ("Rakovina"),[45] and in the poem of that name (26), the shell is specified as one "without pearls." Mandelstam offered only a stone, an ordinary stone that might be picked up anywhere, a stone that a mason could use to build with. The title is also a

---

[42] Gumilyov reviewed both the 1913 and the 1916 editions of *Stone* in *Apollon*: see Gumilyov, 4: 327-328, 363-366. The reviews appeared in *Apollon*, no. 1-2 (January-February 1914) and no. 1 (January 1916).

[43] "Mandelstam," AAS, 2: 167.

[44] Quoted in Zhirmunsky, "Two Tendencies," in Proffer and Proffer, eds., *Silver Age of Russian Culture*, p. 60.

[45] B, p. 161. There is an odd and presumably accidental echo of Wordsworth's vision of the Bedouin carrying a stone and a shell (*Prelude* 5. 71-165). The stone represents reality, the shell vision, and the poet "wondered not, although I plainly saw/The one to be a stone, the other a shell/Nor doubted once but that they both were books" (ll. 111-113).

reference to Fyodor Tyutchev (1803-1873), one of nineteenth-century Russia's greatest poets. Mandelstam revered Tyutchev for his craftmanship and verbal precision, and he often incorporates phrases from Tyutchev in his own poetry. He found the title *Stone* in a poem that Tyutchev wrote in January 1833:

A stone that rolled down off the mountain,
        lies in the valley.
How did it fall? No one knows now—
Did it break away from the summit *by itself*,
Or [was it] hurled down by some *deliberate* hand?[46]

Vladimir Solovyov, the favorite philosopher of the mystical Symbolists, "used to feel a peculiar prophetic terror in the presence of grey Finnish boulders," Mandelstam tells us in "The Morning of Acmeism":

The mute eloquence of the granite block upset him, like malignant witchcraft. But the stone of Tyutchev, which "rolled down off the mountain . . . " is the word. In this unexpected fall, the voice of matter sounds, like articulate speech. One can only respond to this summons with architecture. The Acmeists reverently take up the enigmatic Tyutchevian stone and set it in the foundation of their building.

The stone as it were thirsted for a different mode of existence. It discovered for itself the potentially dynamic power latent in itself—requesting, as it were, to participate in the "cross-vaulting," in the joyful interdependency of its fellows.

For Mandelstam, then, stone was the basic building material, just as the word is the basic building material for a poem, and he saw himself not as a creator but as a

[46] F. I. Tyutchev, *Polnoe sobranie stikhotvorenii* [Complete collected poems], Biblioteka poeta (Leningrad: Sovetskii pisatel', 1957), p. 131. See Mandelstam's quoting of this passage in *Stone* 34, lines 3-4. The underlined words are italicized in the original.

builder. A building is made out of stone; a poem is made out of words, not out of ideas or its subject matter. A word "thirsts" to participate in a poem, for the poem is a new mode of existence, a challenge to the void of silence and nothingness, just as the stone thirsts to participate in the soaring vault that supports roof or tower, to create a structure where only emptiness had been:

> Stone, become a web,
> A lace fragility:
> Let your thin needle stab
> The empty breast of sky.   (29)

"To build means to contend with the void, to hypnotize space," Mandelstam explains. "the beautiful shaft of the Gothic bell tower is angry, for the entire meaning of it is to stab the sky, to reproach it because it is empty."[47]

The stone-word is active, not passive. It is not acted upon by the mason who places it in the arch but rather enters into a strenuous and continual activity, the sustaining of the structure. "The arch never sleeps"[48]—and neither does Mandelstam's line and stanza, in which each word accepts its charge of dynamically sustaining the poem. In a poem of 1933 (SS, poem 276), he describes the creative moment when a poem is achieved:

> How splendid and how oppressive,
> When the moment is drawing nearer—
> And then suddenly the tension of the arch
> Can be heard in my mutterings.

Mandelstam's habit of thinking of poetry in architectural terms often leads him to write poems about build-

---

[47] All prose quotations in the two preceding paragraphs are from "The Morning of Acmeism," SS, 2: 364-65. The "cross-vaulting" is from *Stone* 39, line 3.

[48] This phrase is a kind of refrain in J. Meade Falkner's architectural novel, *The Nebuly Coat* (1903), a novel Mandelstam would probably have liked. See also William Golding's *The Spire* (1964).

ings: "The Admiralty" (48), "Notre Dame" (39), "Hagia Sophia" (38). These poems are at once statements and examples of his poetic creed—especially "The Admiralty," which is about a St. Petersburg building that is literally a word, or at least an initial letter: the central arch forms the Russian letter "П," Peter's initial. The Admiralty was built to emphasize Russia's eagerness to communicate with the West, and above the arch the architect has "quoted" two Western buildings, a classical temple (to Mandelstam an "Acropolis") and above that a Gothic spire. Finally, the poem and the building refute the Symbolist idea of poetry as inspiration, a sudden God-given vision, and teach "that beauty is no demi-god's caprice/ But is caught by a simple carpenter's greedy eye." "Irish poets, learn your trade," Yeats was to command in his valedictory poem, "Sing whatever is well made."

Mandelstam's "Notre Dame" celebrates a monument of Western culture and its Roman origin. The poet does not look at the cathedral romantically, and he does not mention the Virgin at all. His poem is almost aggressively masculine, and he sees the church as "original, exulting,/ Each nerve stretched taut along the light cross-vaulting,/ Each muscle flexing, like Adam when he first woke"— Michelangelo's Adam on the ceiling of the Sistine Chapel, testing his newly discovered powers. The lines evoke Mandelstam's sense that Gothic architecture is "the triumph of dynamics" and that a Gothic cathedral is more in motion and more fluid than a wave in the sea.[49] And they recall that the Acmeists also thought of calling themselves Adamists, the name Sergey Gorodetsky preferred in his manifesto[50]: a poet should look at the world with Adam's fresh eye, and Adam created words by giving names to things.

The cathedral is at once Adam awakening to new creation and an epitome of Western culture and of human his-

[49] "François Villon," SS, 2: 350.
[50] Sergey Gorodetsky, "Some Tendencies in Contemporary Russian Poetry" ("Nekotorye techenìya v sovremennoi russkoi poezii"), *Apollon*, no. 1 (January 1913), pp. 46-50.

tory. When the poet looks at the cathedral, his perception expands through time to include the Gothic age when the church was built, its architectural stresses and strains planned and controlled; then back to an even earlier event, the founding of Paris as a Roman outpost, an extension of Roman law and logic into empty or uncivilized space, which was the necessary preamble to the development of Gothic architectural skills; and then back even further to the creation of Adam, when the Word of God created man to fill the empty spaces of the world, to raise himself erect and make ready to raise cathedrals and towers. If Adam is indeed the Adam of the Sistine Chapel, Rome reenters the poem with him, or rather continues in the poem—Renaissance Rome now, in the most literal sense. Mandelstam would expect his reader to recall the etymology of *tsar*, derived from Caesar, invoking the unity that Rome created for European culture—like the Dante he imagined, he wanted a reader to make "rapid associations . . . grasp things on the wing . . . be sensitive to allusions,"[51] and even catch an echo of Revelation 11: 1: "And there was given me a reed like unto a rod: and the angel stood, saying, Rise, and measure the temple of God." A whole tradition is continuously and insistently present in both cathedral and poem.

"Hagia Sophia" presents another cathedral that embodies its own tradition. Mandelstam admires Justinian for incorporating the ancient Greek past in his building by using pillars from the temple of Diana at Ephesus. He emphasizes the reality of the building, and specifies its elements: 107 pillars, 40 windows, 4 pendentives. The mystical Symbolists had made much of what they called "the Eternal Sophia," a feminine embodiment of Divine Wisdom. Vladimir Solovyov had spent much of his life seeking her—Her?—and had actually glimpsed her on three occasions: in a Moscow church when he was nine, in the British Museum Reading Room, and in the desert near

[51] Dante, p. 68. See also Monas, p. 7; SS, 2: 406.

Cairo[52]; a little later she became Blok's Eternal Feminine, a mysterious and beautiful woman who shows herself only occasionally to the poet, and then only for a moment. On the other hand, Mandelstam's solid church is always there, and visible to all; it is not evoked by an individual sensibility but instead develops out of and directs the religious and cultural aspirations of its society.

Mandelstam's preoccupation with architecture also leads him to write poems about cityscapes, especially poems about St. Petersburg, the city whose name operates as a kind of subtext for the title *Stone*. Petersburg is a city of stone, built of that gray Finnish granite that brought on Solovyov's "prophetic terror." Its name incorporates Christ's only recorded pun, on the word stone: "Tu es Petrus, et super hanc petram aedificabo ecclesiam meam"— "You are Stone, and upon this stone I will build my church." Petersburg—Stone City. When Tsar Peter named his new capital after his own patron saint, he deliberately emphasized the city's "Western" aspects by using non-Russian words—Sankt Peterburg: *Sankt* is Dutch and German, from the Latin *sanctus* (the Russian word would be *svatoi*); Peter rather than Pyotr; and German *burg* instead of Russian *grad*.

Mandelstam's St. Petersburg is not the vague and hallucinatory city of Dostoevsky, of Blok, of Bely's *Petersburg*. It is a real and specific city, caught in a moment of time in "Petersburg Stanzas" (42) much as a photograph or a statue freezes action. The city is literally frozen, the Neva icebound and its ships unmoving. Tsar Peter himself appears but as a statue, the famous "Bronze Horseman" fixed forever upon a granite wave that will never break, forever pointing to the West. The law student of stanza one is caught with his arm in a similar gesture. The city's reality—and its myth—has already been fixed

---

[52] See his poem "Three Meetings" ("Tri svidan'ya," 1898), in *Stikhotvoreniia i shutochnie p'esi* [Poems and comic pieces], Biblioteka poeta (Leningrad: Sovetskii pisatel', 1974), p. 125.

in architecture and literature: the statue and "Queer proud Evgeni" evoke Pushkin's poem *The Bronze Horseman* (*Medny vsadnik*), and Pushkin's Onegin is also present.

St. Petersburg is named for a saint associated with the papacy and Rome, and the two cities are architecturally similar—when the architect of the Kazan Cathedral "quotes" Bernini's colonnade at St. Peter's, Mandelstam refers to him as "a Russian with his heart in Rome" (61). The poet's heart is often in Rome, at once papal and imperial. His attitude toward Rome was influenced by the philosopher Pyotr Chaadaev (1794-1856), who admired Catholicism and Western culture. Mandelstam's interest in Catholicism was cultural rather than theological: he inherited Chaadaev's respect for the papacy as the great unifying principle of Western Europe rather than as a divinely sanctioned religious authority. Rome defines "man's place in the universal scheme" (66) by continuing the Judaeo-Graeco-Roman cultural tradition that was centered on man and man's needs.

Western Europe, together with St. Petersburg and some of the little outposts of the classical world along the Black Sea, exemplified order and form, qualities lacking in the vast sprawl of the Russian landscape that Chaadaev had called raw and undefined.[53] While in his Voronezh exile in 1937, Mandelstam described himself as sick of the open plains (SS, poem 351) and held prisoner by their "lucid dreariness" (SS, poem 352), unable to leave "these hills of Voronezh, still young/For those lucid hills of Tuscany where all men feel at home." The landscape of the West was comfortable, familiar—"I love bourgeois, European comfort and am devoted to it not only physically but also emotionally," he wrote Vyacheslav Ivanov from Switzerland in 1909.[54] The landscape was on a human scale, long habituated to and shaped by a human presence and possessing what Mandelstam called Hellenism:

[53] "Pyotr Chaadaev," SS, 2: 327.
[54] B, p. 37.

Hellenism is a cooking pot, oven tongs, an earthen-
ware jug of milk, household utensils, dishes, all the
things that surround a human body; Hellenism is the
warmth of the hearth recognized as something holy;
it is any possession that connects a man with some
part of the world outside himself. . . . Hellenism is a
man deliberately surrounded with utensils instead of
with indifferent objects, the turning of indifferent ob-
jects into utensils, humanizing the surrounding
world, warming a man with a gentle teleological
warmth. Hellenism is any stove beside which a man
sits and enjoys the warmth as something akin to his
internal warmth. . . . Hellenism is the system, in the
Bergsonian meaning of the word, which a man sets
up around himself.[55]

"Every craft was dear to Mandelstam," his wife tells us,
"because the craftsman makes utensils, fills and domes-
ticates the world."[56] Even during his brief boyhood inter-
est in Marxism, he read Karl Kautsky's *Erfurt Program* as
if it were Tyutchev's poetry, for it enabled him to "popu-
late, to socialize the visible world with its barley, dirt
roads, castles, and sunlit spider webs. . . . I perceived the
entire world as an economy, a human economy—and the
shuttles of English domestic industry that had fallen si-
lent a hundred years ago sounded once more in the ring-
ing autumn air!"[57] From the concentration camp where
he had been imprisoned in 1966 for writing about Man-
delstam and similar crimes, Andrey Sinyavsky admired
Mandelstam's ability to preserve "a sense of meaning in
life . . . of feeling at home in the universe."[58]

Mandelstam criticized the Symbolists because they

[55] "Concerning the Nature of the Word," SS, 2: 295-296.
[56] N. Mandelstam, *Mozart and Salieri*, p. 71.
[57] P, p. 111.
[58] See the transcript of Sinyavsky's trial, *Na skam'e podsudimykh* [In
the Dock] (New York: Inter-Language Literary Associates, 1966); the re-
mark about Mandelstam is from a review by Henry Gifford, *TLS*, 14 June
1977.

would not be domestic. They did not love this world nor feel at home in it. They were transient and ungrateful guests, looking on the world "as a burden and an unfortunate accident" rather than as a "palace which is a gift of God. After all," he asks, "what are you to say about an ungrateful guest, who lives at his host's expense, enjoys his hospitality, and meanwhile despises him in his heart and is thinking only about how to overreach him."[59] Mandelstam's ideal of a physical world in which man could be at ease is one more way of emphasizing the Acmeist commitment to man, to man's world, to reality. Mandelstam quotes Villon: "I know well that I am not the son of an angel, crowned with a diadem from some star or from another planet," and then adds approvingly, "a denial like that is worth the same as a positive assertion."[60] It is a far cry from the Symbolists, who yearned for the stars and enjoyed quoting the passage in which Ivan Karamazov accepted God but rejected His world. Mandelstam's poems are committed to the world we know. When stars appear, they are remote, threatening, inhuman, and Nadezhda Mandelstam says that Mandelstam knew that he had exhausted a poetic impulse whenever he found himself writing about stars.[61]

POETRY AND QUOTATION

Pasternak once remarked that Mandelstam "got into a conversation which was started before" he appeared,[62] the "conversation" being all literature, and indeed all culture. Mandelstam's view of the poet is close to Eliot's in "Tradition and the Individual Talent" (1919): the poet is not a self-made Romantic visionary but part of a cultural continuum. Phrases from older Russian poetry, and sometimes phrases from the work of his contemporaries, are

[59] "The Morning of Acmeism," SS, 2: 364.
[60] "François Villon," SS, 2: 351.
[61] N. Mandelstam, *Hope Against Hope*, pp. 197-198.
[62] N. Mandelstam, *Mozart and Salieri*, p. 22.

audible in Mandelstam's poems. He quotes, as Eliot and Pound quote, to extend the range of his own poems. "A quotation is not an excerpt," he declared. "A quotation is a cicada. It is part of its nature never to quiet down"—and he praises the end of Canto IV of the *Inferno* as "a genuine orgy of quotations . . . a keyboard promenade around the entire mental horizon of antiquity."[63] The forcible abridgment of Russian culture by the Soviet regime, or the comparative inaccessibility of that culture for the English-speaking reader, have blurred some of Mandelstam's references and citations for Russian and non-Russian readers. Some of his poems can seem obscure and solipsistic, but in fact they are as firmly rooted in both an historical and cultural context and in physical reality as Joyce's *Ulysses* or Eliot's *Waste Land*.

In deploying quotations, and in the general organization of a poem, Mandelstam's method is often associative. One image transforms itself into another through the poet's perception of an inner likeness between them, and the metamorphoses of image into image constitute the action of the poem.[64] Mandelstam's description of Henri Bergson is a brief explanation of his own method: "Only the internal relationship of phenomena interests him. He frees this relationship from time and considers it by itself. In this way interrelated phenomena make up, as it were, a fan, the leaves of which can unfold in time, but at the same time it allows itself to be folded up in a way that is intellectually comprehensible."[65] In Poem 60, for example, the shaggy fur-coated men who opened the courtyard gates of Russian houses metamorphose (appropriately enough in a poem about Ovid) into ancient Scythian nomads, as Ovid described them in his *Tristia*.

Mandelstam's "Dombey and Son" (53) is built on associations and has sometimes bothered readers familiar with Dickens's novel and expecting some accurate recapitulation. The poem starts with words and their sounds:

[63] Dante, p. 69. See also Monas, p. 7; SS, 2: 407.

[64] Dante, p. 81. See also Monas, p. 19; SS, 2: 421-422.

[65] "Concerning the Nature of the Word," SS, 2: 284.

the sibilance that Mandelstam believes to be characteristic of spoken English (a language he did not know) makes him think of the sibilant name of Oliver Twist, although he seems not to have read the novel in which Oliver appears. Oliver Twist makes him think of Dickens and specifically of *Dombey and Son*, a novel he clearly has read. For him that novel evokes nineteenth-century London in words, and the reader can experience that London in much the same way as Huysmans' Des Esseintes stays in Paris and experiences England by smelling tar, eating roast beef, and drinking stout. Dickens's power is to make his world physically present for us, and Mandelstam selects a few details: Dombey's office and the clerks who work there; little Paul Dombey, who does not understand, as everyone else does, that his death is near; the invasion of the countinghouse and Dombey's own house, the two nodes of the story, by bailiffs after Dombey's bankruptcy; Florence Dombey's repudiation by her father and their later reconciliation. The poem charts Mandelstam's response to the experienced reality of the novel, shifting unexpectedly from image to image; it reproduces not the novel but Mandelstam's experience of it, and so exists in its own right. In "Talking about Dante" ("Razgovor o Dante"), Mandelstam likens the reading of a poem to a man crossing a Chinese river by leaping from one to another of the junks that are sailing up and down. His route is the logical one under the circumstances, but each leap is taken because of the sudden juxtaposition of one moving junk to another, and so the logic of his progress cannot easily be recovered or charted.[66]

Translating Mandelstam

Working with Mandelstam in the intimacy of translation, I have naturally wondered what he would think of my results. He said many harsh things about translators and

[66] Dante, p. 66. See also Monas, p. 4; SS, 2: 404.

translations in his later years, perhaps because he resented the way in which he had been confined to that literary activity, which became mere drudgery to him. He was himself a gifted translator of verse, as his versions of Petrarch and other poets attest, and unlike many poets, he did believe that poetry could be successfully translated. In a sardonic little poem of 1933 (SS, poem 273), he even professes to believe that the translator gains a special insight into his subject:

> Tartars, Uzbecks, Nenetsians,
> And the whole Ukrainian nation,
> And even the Volga Germans
> Are waiting for translation.
>
> At this very moment,
>   somewhere,
> Perhaps some Japanese is at work
> Boring into my very soul
> As he translates me into Turk.

The present translator claims no such penetration, but to work with Mandelstam's poems and to read Nadezhda Mandelstam's memoir is to feel the presence of an extraordinarily attractive and unified personality, a man absolutely serious about the importance of his profession and true to the binding oath he had taken to it. The values explicit in his poems—clarity, order, respect for man and his needs, precision, the classical tradition, an integrity of the word and therefore of the thought—are values that seem to be continually present in every moment of his life, and they explain why Stalin could not allow him to live. His presence threatened a system based on anarchy and lies. Mandelstam's only explicit political act was his intervention on behalf of some clerks who were about to be executed, by sending Bukharin a copy of the 1928 *Poems* with the inscription, "Every line here is against what you are going to do."[67] The poems still have that ef-

---

[67] N. Mandelstam, *Hope Against Hope*, p. 113.

fect. To work with them is to sense their humanity and to feel privileged for having been allowed the experience.

Mandelstam would have known the essay in which Gumilyov defines the Acmeist theory of translation. Gumilyov's strict requirements can be summarized as a demand that the translator be faithful to his text and not impose either his own ideology or his own personality upon someone else's poetry. He offers nine commandments which list the specific elements in a poem that the translator must preserve, adding drily, "since there is one commandment less than those of Moses, I hope that they will be obeyed better." The translator must retain

1) the number of the lines,
2) the meter and the number of feet,
3) the alternation of the rhymes,
4) the nature of the enjambement,
5) the nature of the rhymes,
6) the character of the vocabulary,
7) the type of comparison or simile,
8) any special mannerisms,
9) the changes of tone.[68]

These are the rules I have tried to follow, insofar as it is possible to do so when translating from an inflected language, with its multiplicity of rhymes, to an uninflected language with a different tradition of what is permissible in the way of metrical variation. I have tried first to be lexically accurate, and next to preserve Mandelstam's rhymes and rhyme schemes, which are essential for a poet committed both to pattern and order and to imposing pattern and order on his verse by using meter and rhyme; a free verse translation of Mandelstam's rhymed verse would be inappropriate, as it would be for Alexander Pope. I have taken comfort—and license—from the theo-

[68] "About the Translating of Poetry" ("O stikhotvornikh perevodakh," 1920), Gumilyov, 4: 190-196. The rules are on page 196. Gumilyov's editors have given the essay its title.

ries of Austin Clarke, who adapted some of the traditional methods of Irish prosody to poetry written in English, and in so doing extended the possibilities for rhymes that are not identical. I have not been able to reproduce Mandelstam's meter in English, line for line and beat for beat. I do not think this is possible, given the different natures of the two languages, and I am not sure that it is even desirable. I have sometimes varied the meter from one stanza to another within a poem to emphasize the way in which a Mandelstam lyric does not develop logically. My line is thus deliberately less regular than his; Gumilyov called on his fellow Acmeists to "break the chains of meter,"[69] while Ezra Pound was freeing poetry in English from those same chains, and a too constant regularity sounds mechanical today.

THE READER

In 1913, Mandelstam wrote an essay about an important literary figure who is often neglected by poets and critics: the reader. Poetry, he tells us, ought to be addressed to some " 'reader in posterity' . . . unknown but definite," and not to a reader sharing the poet's own time, place, and ideas. The air in which a poem "flies" is "the unexpected. Speaking to someone well known we can only say what is well known. . . . But to exchange signals with Mars . . . there is a worthy task for a lyric poet. . . . Poetry taken as a whole is always sent to an addressee who is more or less remote and unknown, an addressee whose real existence the poet cannot doubt, lest he doubt himself."[70] The poet is most on his mettle when he tries to attract the attention and understanding of this remote reader, whose

[69] "The Legacy of Symbolism and Acmeism," Gumilyov, 4: 172. For a useful discussion of Russian prosody, see Vladimir Nabokov, *Notes on Prosody*, in volume 3 (appendix 2) of his translation of *Eugene Onegin*, revised edition (Princeton: Princeton University Press, 1975); the *Notes* have also been published separately.

[70] "Concerning the Interlocutor" ("O sobesednike"), SS, 2: 279-282.

tastes and ideas are unimaginable. Mandelstam's essay is a fascinating discussion of a poet's awareness of his reader and of his reader's needs. But it is also sadly prophetic, as if he foresaw how he was to be prevented from communicating with his own contemporaries and with his own countrymen. Like most of twentieth-century Russia's greatest writers, he has had to find his readers abroad, and often only after translation.

In his essay "Concerning the Nature of the Word," Mandelstam approaches the idea of "the reader in posterity" by creating a striking metaphor. He describes a poem as being like

> the funerary boat of the dead Egyptians, in which they store everything that is needed for carrying on with a man's earthly journey, even a jar of spices, a mirror and a comb. . . .
> The century falls silent, culture goes to sleep, the nation is born again . . . and this whole moving current carries the fragile boat of the human word out into the open sea of the future, where there is no sympathetic understanding, where dismal commentary takes the place of the bracing wind of our contemporaries' hostility and sympathy. How is it possible to fit this boat out for its long voyage if we do not supply it with everything necessary for a reader [in the remote future] who is at once so alien to us and so precious? Again, I compare a poem to an Egyptian ship of the dead. Everything needed for life is stored in this ship, and nothing is forgotten.[71]

A similar "ship of the dead" caught the imagination of D. H. Lawrence when he visited an Etruscan tomb in 1927 and saw "the sacred treasures of the dead, the little bronze ship of death that should bear him over to the other world, the vases of jewels for his arraying, the vases of small dishes, the little bronze statuettes and tools, the

[71] "Concerning the Nature of the Word," SS, 2: 296-301.

armour." For Lawrence the "ship of death" became an important metaphor in the poems he wrote as his own death approached:

> Oh build your ship of death, your little ark
> and furnish it with food, with little cakes, and wine
> for the dark flight down oblivion.
>
> ....
>
> A little ship, with oars and food
> and little dishes, and all accoutrements
> fitting and ready for the departing soul.

In another poem on the same subject, written a little later, Lawrence urged pity for "the dead that were ousted out of life/all unequipped to take the long, long voyage."[72] Mandelstam was ousted from life, but his ship had been prepared; it lay ready, rigged, and equipped. It has already carried him past oblivion and into many alien harbors; someday it will even reach a Russian port.

The Stone House/Teach na gcloch   ROBERT TRACY
Brandon, West Kerry

[72] *The Complete Poems of D. H. Lawrence,* ed. Vivian de Sola Pinto and F. Warren Roberts (New York: Viking, 1971), pp. 18, 718, 722.

STONE

1.

Звук осторожный и глухой
Плода, сорвавшегося с древа,
Среди немолчного напева
Глубокой тишины лесной . . .   1908.

1.

A tentative hollow note
As a pod falls from a tree
In the constant melody
Of the wood's deep quiet . . .   1908.

2.

Сусальным золотом горят
В лесах рождественские елки;
В кустах игрушечные волки
Глазами страшными глядят.

О вещая моя печаль,
О тихая моя свобода
И неживого небосвода
Всегда смеющийся хрусталь!   1908.

2.

In the wood there are Christmas trees
With golden tinsel blazing;
In the thickets toy wolves are gazing
With terrifying eyes.

O my prophetic sadness,
O my silent freedom
And the heavens' lifeless dome
Of eternally laughing glass!   1908.

3.

Из полутемной залы, вдруг,
Ты выскользнула в легкой шали —
Мы никому не помешали,
Мы не будили спящих слуг ...   1908.

3.

In a light shawl, you suddenly slipped
Out of the shadowed hall—
We disturbed no one at all
Nor woke the servants up . . .   1908.

4.

Только детские книги читать,
Только детские думы лелеять,
Все большое далеко развеять,
Из глубокой печали восстать.

Я от жизни смертельно устал,
Ничего от нее не приемлю,
Но люблю мою бедную землю
Оттого, что иной не видал.

Я качался в далеком саду
На простой деревянной качели,
И высокие темные ели
Вспоминаю в туманном бреду.   1908.

4.

To have only a child's books for reading
And only a child's thoughts to nurse,
To let all grown up things disperse,
To rise out of deep grieving.

Life has made me mortally weary;
I will take nothing it gives,
But I love my land, poor as it is,
For I've seen no other country.

In a far away garden I swung
On a plain wooden swing—I recall
Fir trees, mysterious and tall,
In my vague delirium.   1908.

5.

Нежнее нежного
Лицо твое,
Белее белого
Твоя рука,
От мира целого
Ты далека,
И все твое —
От неизбежного.

От неизбежного
Твоя печаль
И пальцы рук
Неостывающих,
И тихий звук
Неунывающих
Речей,
И даль
Твоих очей.   1909.

5.

More delicate than delicacy
Your face,
Whiter than purity
Your hand;
Living as distantly
From the world as you can
And everything about you
As it must be.

It must all be like this:
Your sorrow
And your touch
Never cooling,
And the quiet catch
Of not complaining
In the things you say,
And your eyes
Looking far away.   1909.

6.

На бледно-голубой эмали,
Какая мыслима в апреле,
Березы ветви поднимали
И незаметно вечерели.

Узор отточенный и мелкий,
Застыла тоненькая сетка,
Как на фарфоровой тарелке
Рисунок, вычерченный метко,

Когда его художник милый
Выводит на стеклянной тверди,
В сознании минутной силы,
В забвении печальной смерти.   1909.

6.

Against pale blue enamel, the shade
That only April can bring,
The birch tree's branches swayed
And shyly it was evening.

The pattern, precise and complete,
A network of thinly etched lines
Like the ones on a porcelain plate
With its carefully drawn design,

When the dear artist creates
The design on the glaze's hardness,
At that moment his skill awake,
No thought for death's sadness.   1909.

7.

Есть целомудренные чары —
Высокий лад, глубокий мир,
Далеко от эфирных лир
Мной установленные лары.

У тщательно обмытых ниш
В часы внимательных закатов
Я слушаю моих пенатов
Всегда восторженную тишь.

Какой игрушечный удел,
Какие робкие законы
Приказывает торс точеный
И холод этих хрупких тел!

Иных богов не надо славить:
Они как равные с тобой,
И, осторожною рукой,
Позволено их переставить.   1909.

7.

These spells are austere—
Their harmony is deep, their calm is high;
Far from the starry Lyra in the sky
I have set up my Lares here.

By the well-washed niche where they stand,
At the sunset hour, I listen;
I hear my Penates then,
Constant rhapsody without sound.

How trivial are the fates
And how timid the laws they rule,
These bodies carefully tooled
And the cold of these fragile shapes.

One need not offer other gods prayer;
These are your equals—you may
In a cautious and gentle way
Even shift them here and there.   1909.

8.

Дано мне тело — что мне делать с ним,
Таким единым и таким моим?

За радость тихую дышать и жить,
Кого, скажите, мне благодарить?

Я и садовник, я же и цветок,
В темнице мира я не одинок.

На стекла вечности уже легло
Мое дыхание, мое тепло.

Запечатлеется на нем узор,
Неузнаваемый с недавних пор.

Пускай мгновения стекает муть —
Узора милого не зачеркнуть.   1909.

8.

A body is given to me—what am I to make
From this thing that is my own and is unique?

Tell me who it is I must thank for giving
The quiet joy of breathing and of living?

I am the gardener, the flower as well,
Never alone in the world's prison cell.

My warmth, my breathing have already lain
Upon eternity's clear pane.

Imprinted on the glass a pattern shows,
But nowadays a pattern no one knows.

Let the dregs of the moment drain away—
The pattern's loveliness must stay.   1909.

9.

Невыразимая печаль
Открыла два огромных глаза,
Цветочная проснулась ваза
И выплеснула свой хрусталь.

Вся комната напоена
Истомой — сладкое лекарство!
Такое маленькое царство
Так много поглотило сна.

Немного красного вина,
Немного солнечного мая —
И, тоненький бисквит ломая,
Тончайших пальцев белизна.   1909.

9.

Two huge eyes showed
A sorrow words cannot say,
The crystal poured away
As the flower vase overflowed.

The whole room was deep
In languor—that sweet balm!
Such a tiny realm
To swallow so much sleep.

A little red wine is here
A little May sunlight—
And slender fingers, their white
Breaking a thin *petit-beurre*.   1909.

10.

На перламутровый челнок
Натягивая шелка нити,
О пальцы гибкие, начните
Очаровательный урок!

Приливы и отливы рук —
Однообразные движенья,
Ты заклинаешь, без сомненья,
Какой-то солнечный испуг,

Когда широкая ладонь,
Как раковина пламенея,
То гаснет, к теням тяготея,
То в розовый уйдет огонь!

10.

With a mother-of-pearl shuttle
Weave the silk threads in;
O nimble fingers, begin
The task that weaves a spell.

The hands move left and right
In a never varying motion;
No question that you summon
Something terrible, like sunlight,

When the hand, spread open, glows
Like a shell that flushes crimson;
Now it darkens with shade and then
Glides into fiery rose.   [1909.]

11.

Ни о чем не нужно говорить,
Ничему не следует учить,
И печальна так и хороша
Темная звериная душа:

Ничему не хочет научить,
Не умеет вовсе говорить
И плывет дельфином молодым
По седым пучинам мировым.   1909.

11.

There is no need for speech
And nothing to teach;
How sad, yet beautiful
Is the dark brutal soul.

It has nothing it wants to teach
And lacks even the power of speech,
But like a young dolphin swims
Where the world's gray deeps are dim.　　1909.

12.

Когда удар с ударами встречается
И надо мною роковой,
Неутомимый маятник качается
И хочет быть моей судьбой,

Торопится и грубо остановится,
И упадет веретено —
И невозможно встретиться, условиться,
И уклониться не дано.

Узоры острые переплетаются,
И все быстрее и быстрей
Отравленные дротики взвиваются
В руках отважных дикарей...   1910.

12.

When each stroke blends into the last
And above me the pendulum
Swings tirelessly fatally past
Eager to bring my doom,

It hurries, then stops abruptly
And then the spindle's fall—
No chance to arrange things, to parley,
No escape at all.

Sharp patterns wind out and in
And more and more quickly now
Brave savages raise javelins
Tipped with poison, poised to throw . . .   1910.

13.

Медлительнее снежный улей,
Прозрачнее окна хрусталь,
И бирюзовая вуаль
Небрежно брошена на стуле.

Ткань, опьяненная собой,
Изнеженная лаской света,
Она испытывает лето,
Как бы не тронута зимой;

И, если в ледяных алмазах
Струится вечности мороз,
Здесь — трепетание стрекоз
Быстроживущих, синеглазых.   1910.

13.

The snowy hive more slow,
The window's crystal more clear,
A turquoise veil lies on a chair
Carelessly thrown.

The gauze dazzling itself so much,
Caressed by its own soft glow
It lives in summer, as though
It never felt winter's touch;

And though ice diamonds glide
In the eternally frozen stream,
Here flickering dragonflies gleam,
Alive but an hour, blue-eyed.   1910.

14. SILENTIUM

Она еще не родилась,
Она и музыка и слово,
И потому всего живого
Ненарушаемая связь.

Спокойно дышат моря груди,
Но, как безумный, светел день,
И пены бледная сирень
В мутно-лазоревом сосуде.

Да обретут мои уста
Первоначальную немоту,
Как кристаллическую ноту,
Что от рождения чиста!

Останься пеной, Афродита,
И слово в музыку вернись,
И сердце сердца устыдись,
С первоосновой жизни слито!   1910.

14. SILENTIUM

Her birth is yet to be;
She and word and music are one
And so she maintains unbroken
All life in unity.

The sea's breasts rise gently and fall
But day gleams like a maniac
And the foam is faded lilac
In a cloudy sky-blue bowl.

May my lips discover
What has always been mute,
Like a crystal note
That is newborn and pure.

Aphrodite, remain foam!
Let the word become music again;
My heart, you must spurn hearts
Fused in that from which all things come.   1910.

Слух чуткий парус напрягает,
Расширенный пустеет взор
И тишину переплывает
Полночных птиц незвучный хор.

Я так же беден как природа
И так же прост как небеса,
И призрачна моя свобода,
Как птиц полночных голоса.

Я вижу месяц бездыханный
И небо мертвенней холста;
Твой мир болезненный и странный
Я принимаю, пустота!   1910.

15.

The keen ear is a sail stretched taut,
Eyes are blank from scanning distance
And a choir of night birds fly past
Silently, through silence.

I am as poor as nature
And as simple as the sky;
My freedom is as spectral
As the night birds' cry.

I look at a lifeless moon
And a dead sky of canvas;
Though your world is morbid and alien
I accept it, nothingness!   1910.

Как тень внезапных облаков,
Морская гостья налетела
И, проскользнув, прошелестела
Смущенных мимо берегов.

Огромный парус строго реет;
Смертельно-бледная волна
Отпрянула — и вновь она
Коснуться берега не смеет;

И лодка, волнами шурша,
Как листьями ...   1910.

16.

Like the shadow sudden clouds cast,
A guest drifted in, the sea,
And glided murmurously
Along the uneasy coast.

A huge sail rigidly soars;
A wave breaks deadly white and then
Rears backwards and rears again
Not daring to touch shore;

In the breakers a boat is rustling
Like foliage . . .   1910.

17.

Из омута злого и вязкого
Я вырос, тростинкой шурша,
И страстно, и томно, и ласково
Запретною жизнью дыша.

И никну, никем не замеченный,
В холодный и топкий приют,
Приветственным шелестом встреченный
Коротких осенних минут.

Я счастлив жестокой обидою
И в жизни, похожей на сон,
Я каждому тайно завидую
И в каждого тайно влюблен.   1910.

17.

I grew as a rustling reed
Where the pond is foul and muddy
And with languid and tender greed
Breathe a life forbidden to me.

No one sees me as I sink down
To a cold lair in the mud
With a rustle to bid me welcome
In autumn's brief interlude.

I rejoice in my cruel pain
And in life, which is like a dream,
I secretly envy all men
And in secret love all of them.   1910.

18.

В огромном омуте прозрачно и темно,
И томное окно белеет;
А сердце — отчего так медленно оно
И так упорно тяжелеет?

То всею тяжестью оно идет ко дну,
Соскучившись по милом иле,
То, как соломинка, минуя глубину,
Наверх всплывает без усилий.

С притворной нежностью у изголовья стой
И сам себя всю жизнь баюкай,
Как небылицею, своей томись тоской
И ласков будь с надменной скукой.   1910.

18.

The huge pond's clear blackness shows
A window, languidly white;
Why is my heartbeat so slow
With a constant dragging weight?

So heavy it sinks—it yearns
For the cozy mud, and then
Like a buoyant straw, it returns
And floats on the surface again.

Feign tenderness, stand by the pillow,
Sing your life to sleep till its end,
As in legends, indulge your sorrow,
Treat proud ennui as your friend.   1910.

19.

Душный сумрак кроет ложе,
Напряженно дышет грудь...
Может, мне всего дороже
Тонкий крест и тайный путь.   1910.

19.

Dusk stifles me, lying across
The bed where I strain for breath . . .
Perhaps I prize most a slender cross
And a secret path.   1910

20.

Как кони медленно ступают,
Как мало в фонарях огня!
Чужие люди, верно, знают,
Куда везут они меня.

А я вверяюсь их заботе,
Мне холодно, я спать хочу;
Подбросило на повороте
Навстречу звездному лучу.

Горячей головы качанье
И нежный лед руки чужой,
И темных елей очертанья,
Еще невиданные мной.   1911.

20.

How slowly the horses go,
Lanterns shining so dimly!
These strangers probably know
The place they are taking me.

And I trust myself to their kindness,
I am feeling cold, and I yearn
To sleep; I was left at the turn
To confront the starry brightness.

My feverish head sways
And a strange hand's coolness is tender;
The dark loom of fir trees
Is not yet clear.   1911.

21.

Скудный луч холодной мерою
Сеет свет в сыром лесу.
Я печаль, как птицу серую,
В сердце медленно несу.

Что мне делать с птицей раненой?
Твердь умолкла, умерла.
С колокольни отуманенной
Кто-то снял колокола,

И стоит осиротелая
И немая вышина,
Как пустая башня белая,
Где туман и тишина.

Утро, нежностью бездонное,
Полуявь и полусон —
Забытье неутоленное —
Дум туманный перезвон . . .   1911.

Cold meager rays that sow
Thin light in the dripping forest.
I slowly carry sorrow
Like a gray bird in my breast.

What shall I do with this broken bird?
The dead sky has nothing to say.
Fog has left the bell tower obscured
Where they've taken the bells away.

And the orphaned heights are empty
And fallen still
Like the white abandoned tower
Where fog and silence dwell.

In the morning the long caress
Of half awake and half not—
An endless drowsiness—
The vague chiming of thought . . .   1911.

Воздух пасмурный влажен и гулок;
Хорошо и не страшно в лесу.
Легкий крест одиноких прогулок
Я покорно опять понесу.

И опять к равнодушной отчизне
Дикой уткой взовьется упрек, —
Я участвую в сумрачной жизни
И невинен, что я одинок!

Выстрел грянул. Над озером сонным
Крылья уток теперь тяжелы,
И двойным бытием отраженным
Одурманены сосен стволы.

Небо тусклое с отсветом странным —
Мировая туманная боль —
О позволь мне быть также туманным
И тебя не любить мне позволь.   1911.

22.

Dull humid thundery air;
All's well, there's no fear in the wood.
I will humbly bear my light cross once more,
Walking in solitude.

Like a wild duck, rebuke will again
Fly toward my indifferent country—
I share life's darkness and am not to blame
Because I am solitary.

A shot thundered. Ducks' ponderous wings
Fly over the drowsy pond
And the pine trunks are stunned
By their own mirrored beings.

A strange light, and the sky is dull—
The world's vague sorrow—
Permit me vagueness as well
And let me not love you.   1911.

Сегодня дурной день,
Кузнечиков хор спит
И сумрачных скал сень
Мрачней гробовых плит.

Мелькающих стрел звон
И вещих ворон крик...
Я вижу дурной сон,
За мигом летит миг.

Явлений раздвинь грань,
Земную разрушь клеть,
И яростный гимн грянь,
Бунтующих тайн медь!

О, маятник душ строг,
Качается, глух, прям,
И страстно стучит рок
В запретную дверь к нам...   1911.

23.

Today is a bad day,
The cicada chorus sleeps
And the cliff's dark shadow looms
As dismal as tombs.

The ringing arrows gleam
And ominous ravens cry . . .
I glimpse evil things when I dream—
One by one, flickering by.

Break down the walls of being,
Destroy earth's prison,
Let violent anthems sing
Brazen mysteries of rebellion!

The scale for souls does not err,
It blindly swings to the straight,
And against our locked doors we hear
The impassioned knocking of fate . . .   1911.

24.

Смутно-дышащими листьями
Черный ветер шелестит
И трепещущая ласточка
В темном небе круг чертит.

Тихо спорят в сердце ласковом,
Умирающем моем
Наступающие сумерки
С догорающим лучем.

И над лесом вечереющим
Стала медная луна.
Отчего так мало музыки
И такая тишина?   1911.

24.

With a vague soughing of leaves
A black wind rustles by
And a flickering swallow draws
A circle against dark sky.

In my gently dying heart
There is quiet contending
Between twilight drawing on
And daylight ending.

A copper moon stood above
Woods that night filled with darkness.
Why is there so little music
And why such stillness?   1911.

25.

Отчего душа так певуча
И так мало милых имен,
И мгновенный ритм — только случай,
Неожиданный Аквилон?

Он подымет облако пыли,
Зашумит бумажной листвой
И совсем не вернется — или
Он вернется совсем другой.

О широкий ветер Орфея,
Ты уйдешь в морские края,
И, несозданный мир лелея,
Я забыл ненужное «я».

Я блуждал в игрушечной чаще
И открыл лазоревый грот...
Неужели я настоящий,
И действительно смерть придет?   1911.

Why are there such songs in my soul
And so few dear names?
Why is a moment of rhythm mere chance
As when Aquilon suddenly comes?

It will scatter a cloud of dust,
Make the paper leaves murmur and sway,
And will never come back—or come
Different in every way.

Orphic wind, you blow far and wide;
You will enter the realms of the sea;
As I cherished a world not yet made
I relinquished the useless "I."

I roamed in a miniature forest
And found a grotto the color of sky . . .
Am I real? Do I exist?
And will I really die?   1911.

26. РАКОВИНА

Быть может, я тебе не нужен,
Ночь; из пучины мировой,
Как раковина без жемчужин,
Я выброшен на берег твой.

Ты равнодушно волны пенишь
И несговорчиво поешь;
Но ты полюбишь, ты оценишь
Ненужной раковины ложь.

Ты на песок с ней рядом ляжешь,
Оденешь ризою своей,
Ты неразрывно с нею свяжешь
Огромный колокол зыбей;

И хрупкой раковины стены,
Как нежилого сердца дом,
Наполнишь шопотами пены,
Туманом, ветром и дождем...   1911.

26. SEASHELL

Perhaps, Night, you have no need of me;
I am here on your seacoast, hurled
As a shell without pearls might be
Up out of the depths of the world.

You churn up the waves into froth
Not caring; you sing stubbornly on;
You will love, you will know the worth
Of a useless shell's deception.

You will lie by its side in the sand,
You will draw your cope over the shell
And inseparably with it bind
The surf's great bell.

You will fill the frail shell's rooms,
Like the house of a heart not lived in,
With the whispering of foam,
With mist, with wind, with rain . . .   1911.

27.

О небо, небо, ты мне будешь сниться!
Не может быть, чтоб ты совсем ослепло,
И день сгорел, как белая страница:
Немного дыма и немного пепла!   1911.

Oh sky, sky, I'm going to dream about you!
It can't be that you've gone completely blind,
That the day, like a sheet of blank paper, has burnt through
Leaving only a little smoke and ash behind!   1911.

28.

Я вздрагиваю от холода —
Мне хочется онеметь!
А в небе танцует золото —
Приказывает мне петь.

Томись, музыкант встревоженный,
Люби, вспоминай и плачь,
И, с тусклой планеты брошенный,
Подхватывай легкий мяч!

Так вот она — настоящая
С таинственным миром связь!
Какая тоска щемящая,
Какая беда стряслась!

Что, если, над модной лавкою
Мерцающая всегда,
Мне в сердце длинной булавкою
Опустится вдруг звезда?   1912.

28.

I am trembling with cold—
I want to feel nothing!
But the sky dances with gold—
It orders me to sing.

Yearn, anxious minstrel,
Love, remember, mourn,
And catch the light ball
That a dim planet has thrown.

Here it is—the true linking
To a world of mystery!
Such a dreary aching
And such catastrophe!

What if from above that smart shop
Where it twinkles eternally
A star, like a needle, should drop
And pierce my heart suddenly?   1912.

29.

Я ненавижу свет
Однообразных звезд.
Здравствуй, мой давний бред —
Башни стрельчатой рост!

Кружевом, камень, будь,
И паутиной стань:
Неба пустую грудь
Тонкой иглою рань.

Будет и мой черед —
Чую размах крыла.
Так — но куда уйдет
Мысли живой стрела?

Или, свой путь и срок
Я, исчерпав, вернусь:
Там — я любить не мог,
Здесь — я любить боюсь ...   1912.

29.

I hate the light that shines
From the monotonous stars.
Welcome back, old obsession of mine—
Tower that thins to an arrow of spire!

Stone, become a web,
A lace fragility:
Let your thin needle stab
The empty breast of sky.

My turn will come yet—
I feel the wings spreading.
So be it—but where is the target
Where living thought's arrow is heading?

Perhaps I will come back here
When my path and my time both fade:
I could not love there
And here I am afraid . . .   1912.

30.

Образ твой, мучительный и зыбкий,
Я не мог в тумане осязать.
«Господи!» — сказал я по ошибке,
Сам того не думая сказать.

Божье имя, как большая птица,
Вылетело из моей груди.
Впереди густой туман клубится,
И пустая клетка позади.   1912.

30.

In the mist, I could not come at
Your shifting tormenting shape.
"Lord!" I said, not intending that,
But the word came out by mistake.

From my breast, like a great bird,
God's name flew suddenly.
Up ahead the thick mist stirred
And an empty cage was behind me.   1912.

31.

Нет, не луна, а светлый циферблат
Сияет мне, и чем я виноват,
Что слабых звезд я осязаю млечность?

И Батюшкова мне противна спесь:
«Который час?» его спросили здесь,
А он ответил любопытным: «вечность». 1912.

31.

No, not the moon but a clock dial gleams
For me—and am I to blame
If pale stars look milky to me?

I hate Batyushkov's arrogance:
"What's the time?" they asked him once
And he answered, "Eternity."   1912.

32. ПЕШЕХОД

Я чувствую непобедимый страх
В присутствии таинственных высот,
Я ласточкой доволен в небесах
И колокольни я люблю полет!

И, кажется, старинный пешеход,
Над пропастью, на гнущихся мостках
Я слушаю, как снежный ком растет
И вечность бьет на каменных часах.

Когда бы так! Но я не путник тот,
Мелькающий на выцветших листвах,
И подлинно во мне печаль поет;

Действительно, лавина есть в горах!
И вся моя душа — в колоколах,
Но музыка от бездны не спасет!   1912.

32. SOMEONE WALKING

I feel uncontrollable fear
In the face of mysterious heights;
I rejoice at a swallow in the air
And love a bell tower's upward flight.

Like some traveller of long ago
Crossing gulfs—the bridge sways as he walks—
I listen to the avalanche grow,
Eternity striking on stone clocks.

If it were true! But I'm not the traveller I see
Briefly glimpsed against fading leaves,
And sorrow sings truly in me;

In the peaks a real avalanche rolls
And all my soul is up among the bells,
But from the abyss, music will not save me!   1912.

33. КАЗИНО

Я не поклонник радости предвзятой,
Подчас природа — серое пятно.
Мне, в опьяненьи легком, суждено
Изведать краски жизни небогатой.

Играет ветер тучею косматой,
Ложится якорь на морское дно,
И бездыханная, как полотно,
Душа висит над бездною проклятой.

Но я люблю на дюнах казино,
Широкий вид в туманное окно
И тонкий луч на скатерти измятой;

И, окружен водой зеленоватой,
Когда, как роза, в хрустале вино —
Люблю следить за чайкою крылатой!   1912.

33. THE CASINO

I don't enjoy a pleasure planned in advance,
Nature is a smear of grayness now and then.
When I feel a bit euphoric, I'm condemned
To know the colors of a quiet existence.

The wind is playing with a shaggy cloud,
The anchor sinks to the bottom of the sea,
My soul is hung above the damned abyss
As when a canvas sail hangs lifelessly.

But I love to be out on the dunes at the casino,
The wide views that the murky window shows,
And thin on the crumpled tablecloth the light;

Green water all around on every side;
When wine shows red in the crystal, like a rose—
I love to follow a seagull soaring in flight.   1912.

34.

Паденье — неизменный спутник страха,
И самый страх есть чувство пустоты.
Кто камни к нам бросает с высоты —
И камень отрицает иго праха?

И деревянной поступью монаха
Мощеный двор когда-то мерил ты,
Булыжники и грубые мечты —
В них жажда смерти и тоска размаха...

Так проклят будь готический приют,
Где потолком входящий обморочен
И в очаге веселых дров не жгут!

Немногие для вечности живут,
Но если ты мгновенным озабочен —
Твой жребий страшен и твой дом непрочен! 1912.

34.

A sense of falling always goes with fear,
Fear itself is a feeling of emptiness.
Who is hurling down stones from the heights upon us—
What stone defies the earth that holds it there?

And once you measured out the cloister paving
With the step of a monk, as if your legs were wood,
The paving stones, and dreams that were coarse and crude—
In them a wish for death, a longing for wings—

So let a curse fall on this Gothic cloister
Where he who goes in is hoodwinked by the ceiling
And they burn no cheerful logs on the hearthstone there.

Those who live for eternity are rare,
But if you care only about some transient thing
Your destiny is fearful, your house tottering!   1912.

35. ЦАРСКОЕ СЕЛО

Георгию Иванову.

Поедем в Царское Село!
Свободны, ветрены и пьяны,
Там улыбаются уланы,
Вскочив на крепкое седло . . .
Поедем в Царское Село!

Казармы, парки и дворцы,
А на деревьях — клочья ваты,
И грянут «здравия» раскаты
На крик — «здорово, молодцы!»
Казармы, парки и дворцы . . .

Одноэтажные дома,
Где однодумы-генералы
Свой коротают век усталый,
Читая «Ниву» и Дюма . . .
Особняки — а не дома!

Свист паровоза . . . Едет князь.
В стеклянном павильоне свита! . .
И, саблю волоча сердито,
Выходит офицер, кичась:
Не сомневаюсь — это князь . . .

И возвращается домой —
Конечно, в царство этикета —
Внушая тайный страх, карета
С мощами фрейлины седой,
Что возвращается домой . . .   1912.

35. TSARSKOE SELO

to Georgy Ivanov.

Let's go to Tsarskoe Selo
Where, reckless, unthinking, and free
The lancers grin drunkenly
Vaulting over the saddle-bow . . .
Let's go to Tsarskoe Selo!

Barracks, palaces, parks,
Scraps of gun-wadding caught in the trees
And "Long life" rolling thunderously
In response to "Good day, lads, good work!"
Barracks, palaces, parks . . .

Little villas, only one story,
Where generals of one idea
Read *Niva* or perhaps Dumas
To make the dull days go by . . .
Not villas, they're houses really!

A train whistles—the prince must be near.
There's his staff in the glass arcade . . .
Looking cross, and adjusting his braid,
Sword trailing, an officer appears:
There's no doubt that the prince is here . . .

Passing by on its homeward way
With a gray maid-of-honor's remains
To the kingdom where etiquette reigns
Goes a coach, spreading secret dismay
As she goes on her homeward way . . .   1912.

113

36. ЗОЛОТОЙ

Целый день сырой осенний воздух
Я вдыхал в смятеньи и тоске;
Я хочу поужинать, и звезды
Золотые в темном кошельке!

И дрожа от желтого тумана,
Я спустился в маленький подвал;
Я нигде такого ресторана,
И такого сброда не видал!

Мелкие чиновники, японцы,
Теоретики чужой казны...
За прилавком щупает червонцы
Человек — и все они пьяны.

Будьте так любезны, разменяйте —
Убедительно его прошу —
Только мне бумажек не давайте, —
Трехрублевок я не выношу!

Что мне делать с пьяною оравой?
Как попал сюда я, Боже мой?
Если я на то имею право —
Разменяйте мне мой золотой!   1912.

36. A GOLD PIECE

All day long I was breathing the damp of autumn,
Troubled and gloomy as I drew each breath;
I want my supper now, and stars are golden
Down in my purse's depths.

I shivered in the yellow fog and went
Into a cellar that was small and cramped;
I'd never seen that sort of restaurant
Nor such a crowd of tramps!

Petty clerks, Japanese, and those who are
Experts at spending someone else's fortune . . .
A barman fondles coins behind the bar,
Dead drunk, every one.

"Please, would you change this for me, if you will?"
That's how I ask him, very earnestly;
"But please don't hand me a three-ruble bill—
I can't bear paper money!"

Why am I here among this drunken crew?
My God, what brought me into a place like this?
"Do I not have the right to ask that you
Change my gold piece!"   1912.

37. ЛЮТЕРАНИН

Я на прогулке похороны встретил
Близ протестантской кирки, в воскресенье.
Рассеянный прохожий, я заметил
Тех прихожан суровое волненье.

Чужая речь не достигала слуха,
И только упряжь тонкая сияла,
Да мостовая праздничная глухо
Ленивые подковы отражала.

А в эластичном сумраке кареты,
Куда печаль забилась, лицемерка,
Без слов, без слез, скупая на приветы,
Осенних роз мелькнула бутоньерка.

Тянулись иностранцы лентой черной,
И шли пешком заплаканные дамы,
Румянец под вуалью, и упорно
Над ними кучер правил в даль, упрямый.

Кто б ни был ты, покойный лютеранин, —
Тебя легко и просто хоронили.
Был взор слезой приличной затуманен,
И сдержанно колокола звонили.

И думал я: витийствовать не надо.
Мы не пророки, даже не предтечи,
Не любим рая, не боимся ада,
И в полдень матовый горим, как свечи.   1912.

37. A LUTHERAN

Down near the Protestant chapel, just last Sunday,
I was out for a walk and met a funeral.
I could see as I passed, though my thoughts were far away,
That the stern parishioners were troubled, one and all.

Their foreign speech was meaningless to me
And only the slender reins and harness glowed;
In the Sunday street that stretched away emptily
Reflections of the lazy horseshoes showed.

In the gloom of a carriage, balanced on eager springs,
Hypocrite sadness rode with the curtains closed,
Tearless and wordless, returning no one's greetings,
A buttonhole showing an autumnal rose.

The foreigners' black ribbon straggled by,
Ladies on foot, each with a tear-stained face,
Ruddy cheeks under every veil; coachmen sat high
Implacably driving toward some distant place.

Whoever, whatever you were, late Lutheran,
They laid you away smoothly, simply, and well.
Eyes were cast down and decorously ran
And there was a measured tolling of the bell.

No need, I thought, for a flowery oration.
We are not prophets nor do we prepare the way;
We do not love heaven, do not fear damnation,
And we burn without light, like candles at midday.   1912.

38. АЙЯ-СОФИЯ

Айя-София — здесь остановиться
Судил Господь народам и царям!
Ведь купол твой, по слову очевидца,
Как на цепи подвешен к небесам.

И всем векам — пример Юстиниана,
Когда похитить для чужих богов
Позволила Эфесская Диана
Сто семь зеленых мраморных столбов.

Но что же думал твой строитель щедрый,
Когда, душой и помыслом высок,
Расположил апсиды и экседры,
Им указав на запад и восток?

Прекрасен храм, купающийся в мире,
И сорок окон — света торжество;
На парусах, под куполом, четыре
Архангела прекраснее всего.

И мудрое сферическое зданье
Народы и века переживет,
И серафимов гулкое рыданье
Не покоробит темных позолот.   1912.

38. HAGIA SOPHIA

Hagia Sophia—here the Lord ordained
That nations and emperors must halt!
Your dome, say travellers, hangs as if a chain
Held it suspended from the heavens' vault.

Justinian set a standard for all time;
From Ephesus, great Diana let him take
One hundred and seven pillars from her shrine,
Green marble pillars, for his new gods' sake.

What thought your architect, that lavish man,
When, with his concepts and his spirits high,
He set out apse and exedrae to plan,
Ordering which to east and which to west should lie?

A glorious temple floating in the world
With forty windows, each exalting light;
Beneath the dome four pendentives unfurled
Show four Archangels, a resplendent sight.

It is both spherical and wise, a building
That will survive nations and centuries,
And weeping seraphim, with echoing cries,
Will never mar the brightness of the gilding.   1912.

39. NOTRE DAME

Где римский судия судил чужой народ —
Стоит базилика, и радостный и первый,
Как некогда Адам, распластывая нервы,
Играет мышцами крестовый легкий свод.

Но выдает себя снаружи тайный план:
Здесь позаботилась подпружных арок сила,
Чтоб масса грузная стены не сокрушила,
И свода дерзкого бездействует таран.

Стихийный лабиринт, непостижимый лес,
Души готической рассудочная пропасть,
Египетская мощь и христианства робость,
С тростинкой рядом — дуб, и всюду царь — отвес.

Но чем внимательней, твердыня Notre Dame,
Я изучал твои чудовищные ребра,
Тем чаще думал я: из тяжести недоброй
И я когда-нибудь прекрасное создам.   1912.

39. NOTRE DAME

Where a Roman judge framed laws for an alien folk
A basilica stands, original, exulting,
Each nerve stretched taut along the light cross-vaulting,
Each muscle flexing, like Adam when he first woke.

If you look from outside you grasp the hidden plan:
Strong saddle-girth arches watchfully forestall
The ponderous mass from shattering the wall
And hold in check the bold vault's battering ram.

A primal labyrinth, a wood past men's understanding,
The Gothic spirit's rational abyss,
Brute strength of Egypt and a Christian meekness,
Thin reed beside oak, and the plumb line everywhere king.

Stronghold of Notre Dame, the more my attentive eyes
Studied your gigantic ribs and frame
Then the more often this reflection came:
From cruel weight, I too will someday make beauty rise.   1912.

Мы напряженного молчанья не выносим —
Несовершенство душ обидно, наконец!
И в замешательстве уж объявился чтец,
И радостно его приветствовали: просим!

Я так и знал, кто здесь присутствовал незримо:
Кошмарный человек читает Улялюм.
Значенье — суета, и слово — только шум,
Когда фонетика — служанка серафима.

О доме Эшеров Эдгара пела арфа,
Безумный воду пил, очнулся и умолк.
Я был на улице. Свистел осенний шелк, —
И горло греет шелк щекочущего шарфа...   1912

40.

We cannot stand the strain of awkward silence—
After all, it annoys us when a soul is not right.
And in the general confusion, a man stepped out to recite;
They welcomed him with joyful cries: "Commence!"

An invisible man was standing there—I knew him:
A nightmare man was reading "Ulalume."
Meaning is vanity and words mere sound
When phonetics are handmaid to the seraphim.

Edgar sang of the House of Usher on his harp,
The madman drank water, came to himself, stood dumb.
I was out on the street. The silken whistle of autumn—
And warm round my throat, a tickle of silken scarf . . .   1912.

123

41. СТАРИК

Уже светло, поет сирена
В седьмом часу утра.
Старик, похожий на Верлена, —
Теперь твоя пора!

В глазах лукавый или детский
Зеленый огонек;
На шею нацепил турецкий
Узорчатый платок.

Он богохульствует, бормочет
Несвязные слова;
Он исповедоваться хочет —
Но согрешить сперва.

Разочарованный рабочий
Иль огорченный мот —
А глаз, подбитый в недрах ночи,
Как радуга цветет.

Так, соблюдая день субботний,
Плетется он, когда
Глядит из каждой подворотни
Веселая беда;

А дома — руганью крылатой,
От ярости бледна,
Встречает пьяного Сократа
Суровая жена!   1913.

41. AN OLD MAN

Dawn already—a singing siren
Signals seven a.m.
Old man, you who look like Verlaine,
Your time has come.

Childishness in his eyes, or mischief,
Makes a greenish glitter of light;
A patterned Turkish kerchief
Is around his throat, tied tight.

He mutters a blasphemous curse,
Some incoherent confusion;
He wants to confess, but first
He wants to sin.

A workman whose plans went awry
Or a prodigal brought low—
Late last night someone blackened his eye
And it shines now like a rainbow.

Keeping holy the Sabbath day
He shuffles himself past where
From each and every doorway
Vivacious disasters stare.

And so he takes himself home;
Curses fly and his wife is stern,
Pale with rage as she waits to welcome
Drunken Socrates' return.   1913.

42. ПЕТЕРБУРГСКИЕ СТРОФЫ

Н. Гумилеву.

Над желтизной правительственных зданий
Кружилась долго мутная метель,
И правовед опять садится в сани,
Широким жестом запахнув шинель.

Зимуют пароходы. На припеке
Зажглось каюты толстое стекло.
Чудовищна, как броненосец в доке, —
Россия отдыхает тяжело.

А над Невой — посольства полумира,
Адмиралтейство, солнце, тишина!
И государства жесткая порфира,
Как власяница грубая, бедна.

Тяжка обуза северного сноба —
Онегина старинная тоска;
На площади сената — вал сугроба,
Дымок костра и холодок штыка . . .

Черпали воду ялики, и чайки
Морские посещали склад пеньки,
Где, продавая сбитень или сайки,
Лишь оперные бродят мужики.

Летит в туман моторов вереница;
Самолюбивый, скромный пешеход —
Чудак Евгений — бедности стыдится,
Бензин вдыхает и судьбу клянет!

1913.

42. PETERSBURG STANZAS

for N. Gumilyov.

Above the yellow loom of government buildings
The swirling snow fell thick all through the day;
Pulling his overcoat close, a law student swings
His arm out wide, and settles back in his sleigh.

Steamers are moored until spring. Where the sun is hot
The thick glass of cabin windows glows.
Russia, like some enormous dreadnaught,
Lies at her dock in ponderous repose.

The Neva has embassies from half the globe,
The sun, the Admiralty, and silence.
And the state is wearing a stiff purple robe
As poor as a hair shirt worn for penitence.

The heavy weight a northern snob must bear—
The ancient burden of Onegin's anguish;
The wave of a snowdrift on the Senate Square,
Smoke from a fire, a bayonet's cold flash . . .

Skiffs scoop the water, and the gulls
Swoop down to gather on the rigging warehouse
Where *muzhiks* wander, selling spiced drinks and rolls,
As if they were an operetta chorus.

A line of motors rushes through the haze;
Ashamed of his poverty, his walk sedate,
Queer proud Evgeni, with his absurd ways,
Breathes gasoline and curses at his fate.   1913.

43.

„Hier stehe ich — ich kann nicht anders„

«Здесь я стою — я не могу иначе»,
Не просветлеет темная гора —
И кряжистого Лютера незрячий
Витает дух над куполом Петра.   1913.

43.

"Hier stehe ich—ich kann nicht anders."
"Here I stand—I cannot do otherwise,"
Will not illuminate the mountain's gloom—
And the blind soul of sturdy Luther flies
High over Peter's dome.   1913.

44.

От легкой жизни мы сошли с ума.
С утра вино, а вечером похмелье.
Как удержать напрасное веселье,
Румянец твой, о пьяная чума?

В пожатьи рук мучительный обряд,
На улицах ночные поцелуи,
Когда речные тяжелеют струи,
И фонари как факелы горят.

Мы смерти ждем, как сказочного волка,
Но я боюсь, что раньше всех умрет
Тот, у кого тревожно-красный рот
И на глаза спадающая челка.   1913, ноябрь.

44.

We went insane from living indulgently.
Wine before noon, by evening a heavy head.
How can we sustain your feverish red
O drunken plague, and your vain revelry?

The ritual of shaking hands is agony,
Kissing out on the streets at night,
The river's current drifting sluggishly,
And street lamps glaring like torchlight.

In old stories they wait for the wolf; we wait to die,
And I fear that the dying among us will begin
With that fellow there, of the twitching scarlet grin
And the fringe of hair dangling across his eye.

November 1913.

...Дев полуночных отвага
И безумных звезд разбег,
Да привяжется бродяга,
Вымогая на ночлег.

Кто, скажите, мне сознанье
Виноградом замутит,
Если явь — Петра созданье,
Медный Всадник и гранит?

Слышу с крепости сигналы,
Замечаю, как тепло.
Выстрел пушечный в подвалы,
Вероятно, донесло.

И гораздо глубже бреда
Воспаленной головы
Звезды, трезвая беседа,
Ветер западный с Невы.   1913.

45.

. . . The courage of midnight girls
And meteors in reckless flight;
A tramp clutches my coat—do I have
The price of a bed for the night?

Tell me who will deaden
My consciousness with wine,
If reality is Peter's creation:
The granite, the Bronze Horseman?

I hear the salute from the fort
And I notice how warm it grows;
They could probably hear the report
There in the cellars below.

And beneath the incoherence
Of my feverish brain
Are stars and talk that makes sense,
The wind west off the Neva again.   1913.

46. БАХ

Здесь прихожане дети праха
И доски вместо образов,
Где мелом Себастьяна Баха
Лишь цифры значатся псалмов.

Разноголосица какая
В трактирах буйных и церквах,
А ты ликуешь, как Исайя,
О рассудительнейший Бах!

Высокий спорщик, неужели,
Играя внукам свой хорал,
Опору духа в самом деле
Ты в доказательстве искал?

Что звук? Шестнадцатые доли,
Органа многосложный крик,
Лишь воркотня твоя, не боле,
О несговорчивый старик!

И лютеранский проповедник
На черной кафедре своей
С твоими, гневный собеседник,
Мешает звук своих речей.   1913.

46. BACH

They are children of dust who worship here:
Plain boards instead of icons
Where Bach's psalms appear
Only as numbers, chalked on.

We hear such cacophonous noises
From clamorous taverns or church;
You rejoice as Isaiah rejoices,
With exuberant logic, O Bach!

Is it true, great debater, when you
Played your grandsons your chorale
You were seeking in fact to show
That logic is nourished by the soul?

What is sound? Sixteen halftones combine
In the organ's polyphonous roar;
All we hear is how you complain—
What a stiff-necked old fellow you are!

And now the Lutheran preacher
In his black pulpit blends
His sermon, O angry debater,
Into your sounds.   1913.

В спокойных пригородах снег
Сгребают дворники лопатами;
Я с мужиками бородатыми
Иду, прохожий человек.

Мелькают женщины в платках
И тявкают дворняжки шалые,
И самоваров розы алые
Горят в трактирах и домах.   1913.

47.

Yardmen with shovels are working
In quiet suburbs of snow;
Among bearded *muzhiks* I go,
A man passing by, out walking.

Shawled women flit to and fro,
Mongrels yap in a silly way
And houses and bars display
The samovar's rose red glow.   1913.

48. АДМИРАЛТЕЙСТВО

В столице северной томится пыльный тополь,
Запутался в листве прозрачный циферблат,
И в темной зелени фрегат или акрополь
Сияет издали, воде и небу брат.

Ладья воздушная и мачта-недотрога,
Служа линейкою преемникам Петра,
Он учит: красота не прихоть полубога,
А хищный глазомер простого столяра.

Нам четырех стихий приязненно господство;
Но создал пятую свободный человек.
Не отрицает ли пространства превосходство
Сей целомудренно построенный ковчег?

Сердито лепятся капризные медузы,
Как плуги брошены, ржавеют якоря —
И вот разорваны трех измерений узы
И открываются всемирные моря.   1913.

48. THE ADMIRALTY

A dusty poplar droops in the north's metropolis,
A clock's clear dial is tangled in the tree;
Through the dark green leaves a frigate or acropolis
Gleams in the distance, brother to sky and sea.

An airborne ship and a mast too high to reach
Offer Peter's heirs a rule to measure by,
Teaching that beauty is no demigod's caprice
But is caught by a simple carpenter's greedy eye.

Four elements rule us, and their rule is benign,
But then man made a fifth, for man is free.
Does this ark perhaps, with its austere design,
Deny to space its old supremacy?

Capricious medusae, furiously clinging,
And anchors stand rusting like abandoned plows—
Our three dimensional cage is shattering,
All the seas of the world are opening for us now.   1913.

49.

В таверне воровская шайка
Всю ночь играла в домино.
Пришла с яичницей хозяйка;
Монахи выпили вино.

На башне спорили химеры —
Которая из них урод?
А утром проповедник серый
В палатки призывал народ.

На рынке возятся собаки,
Менялы щелкает замок.
У вечности ворует всякий,
А вечность — как морской песок:

Он осыпается с телеги —
Не хватит на мешки рогож,
И недовольный, о ночлеге
Монах рассказывает ложь!   1913.

A gang of thieves in a tavern
Played dominoes until dawn.
The hostess brought an omelette in;
Monks were drinking wine.

Gargoyles argued up on the tower—
Which was most frightful of all?
In the morning a stupid preacher
Summoned the folk to his stall.

On the square the dogs are playful,
The click of a coin-changer's key;
Eternity is plundered by all
But eternity is like sand from the sea,

Trickling down at a wagon's tail—
Too few mats to wrap the bags right;
A monk tells a slanderous tale
Of how poorly he lodged last night.   1913.

50. КИНЕМАТОГРАФ

Кинематограф. Три скамейки.
Сентиментальная горячка.
Аристократка и богачка
В сетях соперницы-злодейки.

Не удержать любви полета:
Она ни в чем не виновата!
Самоотверженно, как брата,
Любила лейтенанта флота.

А он скитается в пустыне —
Седого графа сын побочный.
Так начинается лубочный
Роман красавицы-графини.

И в исступленьи, как гитана,
Она заламывает руки.
Разлука. Бешеные звуки
Затравленного фортепьяно.

В груди доверчивой и слабой
Еще достаточно отваги
Похитить важные бумаги
Для неприятельского штаба.

И по каштановой аллее
Чудовищный мотор несется,
Стрекочет лента, сердце бьется
Тревожнее и веселее.

50. SILENT MOVIE

Silent movie. Three benches for seats.
Sentiment at a feverish pitch.
A lady, well-born and rich
In her evil rival's nets.

Do not restrain love's flight:
She is totally innocent!
She loved the naval lieutenant
Selflessly, as a sister might.

But he's lost in the wilderness—
Bastard son of a grizzled count.
So begins this cheap vulgar account,
The romance of a lovely countess.

Like a gypsy, she wrings her hands
And hysterically waves farewell
As the violent discords swell
From the tortured baby grand.

She still has courage enough,
Though at heart she is guileless and weak,
To discover a way to sneak
The plans to the enemy staff.

Down a road lined with chestnut trees
An enormous motor speeds past,
The film clatters—each heart beats fast
With delight and anxiety.

В дорожном платье, с саквояжем,
В автомобиле и в вагоне,
Она боится лишь погони,
Сухим измучена миражем.

Какая горькая нелепость:
Цель не оправдывает средства!
Ему — отцовское наследство,
А ей — пожизненная крепость.   1913.

By motor and railway carriage,
With a satchel, in travelling suit,
She is only afraid of pursuit,
Worn out by an empty mirage.

The ending is silly and bitter:
It does not justify the means!
For him—his father's demesne,
But a lifetime in prison for her.   1913.

51. ТЕННИС

Средь аляповатых дач,
Где шатается шарманка,
Сам собой летает мяч,
Как волшебная приманка.

Кто, смиривший грубый пыл,
Облеченный в снег альпийский,
С резвой девушкой вступил
В поединок олимпийский?

Слишком дряхлы струны лир:
Золотой ракеты струны
Укрепил и бросил в мир
Англичанин вечно-юный!

Он творит игры обряд,
Так легко вооруженный,
Как аттический солдат,
В своего врага влюбленный!

Май. Грозовых туч клочки.
Неживая зелень чахнет.
Всё моторы и гудки —
И сирень бензином пахнет.

Ключевую воду пьет
Из ковша спортсмен веселый;
И опять война идет,
И мелькает локоть голый!   1913.

51. TENNIS

Summer cabins with rough log walls
Where a hand organ's quavers rise;
Flying high on its own, a ball
Magically lures as it flies.

Who is this, his coarse passion cooled
Under garments of Alpine snow,
Who begins an Olympic duel
With a sportive maid as his foe?

The lyre strings were worn and split;
The Englishman cannot grow old:
He put strings on a golden racket
And tossed it into the world.

He performs the rites of the game
With his fragile weaponry—
Attic warriors were just the same,
Each in love with his enemy.

It is May. Scraps of black cloud
Cast a blight upon everything green.
Motors everywhere, horns too loud,
Lilacs reeking of gasoline.

Now the jolly sportsman drains
A dipper filled at the spring;
Then the battle is joined again,
A bare arm flashing.   1913.

52. АМЕРИКАНКА

Американка в двадцать лет
Должна добраться до Египта,
Забыв «Титаника» совет,
Что спит на дне мрачнее крипта.

В Америке гудки поют,
И красных небоскребов трубы
Холодным тучам отдают
Свои прокопченные губы.

И в Лувре океана дочь
Стоит, прекрасная как тополь;
Чтоб мрамор сахарный толочь,
Влезает белкой на Акрополь.

Не понимая ничего,
Читает «Фауста» в вагоне
И сожалеет, отчего
Людовик больше не на троне.   1913.

52. AN AMERICAN GIRL

An American girl, aged twenty,
She has to go to Egypt,
Ignoring *Titanic*'s warning
Asleep on the bottom, darker than a crypt.

In America, factory whistles hoot
And red skyscraper stacks
Offer cold clouds a salute
With lips that are smoked black.

And in the Louvre Ocean's daughter
Is standing, fair as a poplar;
She runs squirrel-like up Acropolis to loiter
Over marble that looks like sugar.

Understanding nothing at all
She reads *Faust* on the train
And it saddens her to recall
That King Louis no longer reigns.   1913.

53. ДОМБИ И СЫН

Когда, пронзительнее свиста,
Я слышу английский язык —
Я вижу Оливера Твиста
Над кипами конторских книг.

У Чарльза Диккенса спросите,
Что было в Лондоне тогда:
Контора Домби в старом Сити
И Темзы желтая вода.

Дожди и слезы. Белокурый
И нежный мальчик Домби-сын;
Веселых клерков каламбуры
Не понимает он один.

В конторе сломанные стулья,
На шиллинги и пенсы счет;
Как пчелы, вылетев из улья,
Роятся цифры круглый год.

А грязных адвокатов жало
Работает в табачной мгле —
И вот, как старая мочала,
Банкрот болтается в петле.

На стороне врагов законы:
Ему ничем нельзя помочь!
И клетчатые панталоны,
Рыдая, обнимает дочь.

1913.

53. DOMBEY AND SON

When I hear the English tongue
Like a whistle, but even shriller—
I see Oliver Twist among
A heaping of office ledgers.

Go ask Charles Dickens this,
How it was in London then:
The old City with Dombey's office,
The yellow waters of the Thames.

The falling rain and tears.
A fair delicate boy, Dombey's son;
He alone does not grasp what he hears
When the jolly clerks make their puns.

Office chairs falling apart,
The counting of pence and shillings;
All year round, like bees that depart
From a hive, the zeroes are swarming.

And the dirty lawyers' sting
Is at work in a fog of tobacco—
The bankrupt hangs in a noose, to swing
Like worn-out rags, to and fro.

The laws side with his enemies:
Nothing can save him from ruin!
His daughter weeps on her knees
Embracing his checked pantaloons.   1913.

54.

Отравлен хлеб и воздух выпит.
Как трудно раны врачевать!
Иосиф, проданный в Египет,
Не мог сильнее тосковать!

Под звездным небом бедуины,
Закрыв глаза и на коне,
Слагают вольные былины
О смутно пережитом дне.

Немного нужно для наитий:
Кто потерял в песке колчан,
Кто выменял коня — событий
Рассеивается туман;

И если подлинно поется
И полной грудью — наконец
Всё исчезает: остается
Пространство, звезды и певец!   1913.

54.

Air sucked dry, bread turning to mould.
Hard even to doctor a sore!
Joseph in Egypt, after he had been sold,
Could hardly have grieved more.

On horseback under the starry sky
The bedouin closes his eyes and sings
A loose rambling balladry
Of the day's vague happenings.

His themes are ready to hand:
Somebody bartered a steed
Or lost a quiver in the sand—
The hazy events recede;

And if the song is sung truly
With a whole heart, all else disappears
And nothing remains, but only
The singer, space, the stars.   1913.

55.

Летают Валькирии, поют смычки.
Громоздкая опера к концу идет.
С тяжелыми шубами гайдуки
На мраморных лестницах ждут господ.

Уж занавес наглухо упасть готов;
Еще рукоплещет в райке глупец;
Извозчики пляшут вокруг костров.
Карету такого-то! Разъезд. Конец.   1913.

55.

The fiddles play, Valkyries take to the air.
The ponderous opera reaches its final notes.
Footmen are waiting on the marble stair
Holding their masters' cumbersome fur coats.

The final curtain is about to drop;
Some fool in the gallery still claps his hands;
Around their bonfires, cabmen stamp and hop.
Somebody's carriage! Off they go. The end.   1913.

56.

Поговорим о Риме — дивный град!
Он утвердился купола победой.
Послушаем апостольское credo:
Несется пыль и радуги висят.

На Авентине вечно ждут царя —
Двунадесятых праздников кануны —
И строго-канонические луны
Не могут изменить календаря.

На дольный мир бросает пепел бурый
Над форумом огромная луна,
И голова моя обнажена —
О холод католической тонзуры!   1913.

56.

Let's talk of Rome—the marvellous city!
The dome's triumph has made her complete.
Let us hear the Apostles' Creed.
Rainbows hover and dust swirls by.

On Aventine they still wait for a tsar—
Through the Twelve Feasts' vigils—
And moons that are strictly canonical
Cannot alter the calendar.

Brown ash pours down upon this lower world
From a vast moon, above the Forum there,
And my head has been shaved bare—
Ah, this Catholic tonsure feels so cold!   1913.

57. 1 9 1 3

Ни триумфа, ни войны!
О железные, доколе
Безопасный Капитолий
Мы хранить осуждены?

Или римские перуны —
Гнев народа — обманув,
Отдыхает острый клюв
Той ораторской трибуны;

Или возит кирпичи
Солнца дряхлая побозка,
И в руках у недоноска
Рима ржавые ключи?   1914.

57. 1913

No triumphs and no war!
O iron ones, how long must we serve,
We who are condemned to preserve
The Capitol secure?

Have the thunderbolts of Rome—
The people's wrath—been tricked?
Do those sharp beaks rest that are fixed
On the orators' tribune?

Or does the sun's battered wagon
Carry bricks of dried clay
And are Rome's rusty keys
Held by one prematurely born?   1914.

... На луне не растет
Ни одной былинки;
На луне весь народ
Делает корзинки —
Из соломы плетет
Легкие корзинки.

На луне — полутьма,
И дома опрятней;
На луне не дома —
Просто голубятни.
Голубые дома —
Чудо-голубятни...   1914.

No grass grows on the moon,
Not even a single blade;
All the people on the moon
Are in the basket-weaving trade—
Light baskets woven
Out of straw braid.

Twilight the whole day through
And the houses are clean there;
No houses though—it's true
They're dovecotes, nothing more.
Houses of birds' egg blue—
Remarkable dovecotes they are . . .   1914.

59.

Вполоборота, о печаль,
На равнодушных поглядела.
Спадая с плеч, окаменела
Ложноклассическая шаль.

Зловещий голос — горький хмель —
Души расковывает недра:
Так — негодующая Федра —
Стояла некогда Рашель.   *1914*

59. [AKHMATOVA]

Oh sorrow—she half turned around
And eyed the indifferent throng.
Her shawl, almost classical, hung
From her shoulders and turned to stone.

Drunk with pain—voice foreboding to say
Things that burst from her deepest soul:
Acting angry Phèdre's role
Rachel used to stand that way.   1914.

60.

О временах простых и грубых
Копыта конские твердят.
И дворники в тяжелых шубах
На деревянных лавках спят.

На стук в железные ворота
Привратник, царственно-ленив,
Встал, и звериная зевота
Напомнила твой образ, скиф!

Когда, с дряхлеющей любовью
Мешая в песнях Рим и снег,
Овидий пел арбу воловью
В походе варварских телег.   1914.

60.

Horses' hooves tell over and over
Of times that were simple and rude.
Gatekeepers, bulky in fur,
Are sleeping on benches of wood.

When a knock made the iron gate ring
The gatekeeper's bestial gape
As he rose like an indolent king—
Scyth, he evoked your shape!

When with love growing old in his heart,
Mixing Rome and the snow in his song,
Ovid sang of the bullock-drawn cart
In the marching barbarian throng.   1914.

61.

На площадь выбежав, свободен
Стал колоннады полукруг —
И распластался храм Господень,
Как легкий крестовик-паук.

А зодчий не был итальянец,
Но русский в Риме; ну так что ж!
Ты каждый раз как иностранец
Сквозь рощу портиков идешь;

И храма маленькое тело
Одушевленнее стократ
Гиганта, что скалою целой
К земле беспомощно прижат!   1914.

61.

After it had run out into the square
The crescent of the colonnade stood free—
The temple of the Lord was stretched out there
With a garden spider's light fragility.

And the architect was not from Italy
But a Russian with his heart in Rome—what then?
Each time you walk amid the grove of columns
You feel just like a foreigner again.

And the small body of the temple has
A hundred times the more vitality
Than that gigantic rock with all its mass
Pressed down upon the earth there helplessly.   1914.

62.

Есть иволги в лесах, и гласных долгота
В тонических стихах единственная мера.
Но только раз в году бывает разлита
В природе длительность, как в метрике Гомера.

Как бы цезурою зияет этот день:
Уже с утра покой и трудные длинноты;
Волы на пастбище, и золотая лень
Из тростника извлечь богатство целой ноты.   1914.

62.

Orioles in the woods, and the only measure
In tonic verse is to know short vowels from long.
There's a brimming over once in each year, when nature
Slowly draws itself out, like the meter in Homer's song.

This is a day that yawns like a caesura:
Quiet since dawn, and wearily drawn out;
Oxen at pasture, golden indolence to draw
From a pipe of reeds the richness of one full note.   1914.

«Мороженно!» Солнце. Воздушный бисквит.
Прозрачный стакан с ледяною водою.
И в мир шоколада с румяной зарею,
В молочные Альпы мечтанье летит.

Но, ложечкой звякнув, умильно глядеть,
Чтоб в тесной беседке, средь пыльных акаций,
Принять благосклонно от булочных граций
В затейливой чашечке хрупкую снедь...

Подруга шарманки, появится вдруг
Бродячего ледника пестрая крышка —
И с жадным вниманием смотрит мальчишка
В чудесного холода полный сундук.

И боги не ведают — что он возьмет:
Алмазные сливки иль вафлю с начинкой?
Но быстро исчезнет под тонкой лучинкой,
Сверкая на солнце, божественный лед.   1914.

"Ice cream!" Sun. Light airy cakes.
A clear glass tumbler of water, icy cold.
Our dreams take flight, into a chocolate world
Of rosy dawns on milky Alpine peaks.

But as the teaspoon tinkles, it is sweet
In some little summerhouse amid the dry acacias,
To gaze, then take gratefully from tearoom Graces,
Little whorled cups with crumbly things to eat . . .

The street-organ's playmate suddenly appears,
The ice-cream cart, with multicolored covering—
The chest is full of lovely frozen things;
With greedy attentiveness, a small boy peers.

And what will he choose? The gods themselves can't say:
A diamond tart? A wafer filled with cream?
But under his slender spoon the divine ice,
Glittering in the sun, will soon melt away.   1914.

64.

Есть ценностей незыблемая ска́ла
Над скучными ошибками веков.
Неправильно наложена опала
На автора возвышенных стихов.

И вслед за тем, как жалкий Сумароков
Пролепетал заученную роль,
Как царский посох в скинии пророков,
У нас цвела торжественная боль.

Что делать вам в театре полуслова
И полумаск, герои и цари?
И для меня явленье Озерова —
Последний луч трагической зари.   1914.

64.

The scale for values does not change, but stands
Above the dull mistakes of other times
That scorned, because they did not understand,
A poet who had made his verse sublime.

And after Sumarokov in shy misery
Had learned his role, then rattled off his lines,
Pain flowered for us in solemnity
As the prophet's holy staff flowered in the shrine.

In a theater that only hints, what can be done
When a mask is half concealing king or hero?
To me, Ozerov seems the setting sun,
One final ray as tragedy sank low.   1914.

Природа — тот же Рим и отразилась в нем.
Мы видим образы его гражданской мощи
В прозрачном воздухе, как в цирке голубом,
На форуме полей и в колоннаде рощи.

Природа — тот же Рим, и, кажется, опять
Нам незачем богов напрасно беспокоить:
Есть внутренности жертв, чтоб о войне гадать,
Рабы, чтобы молчать, и камни, чтобы строить!   1914.

Nature is the same as Rome, and mirrored there.
We can see the forms of civic power displayed:
The sky like a circus in the lucid air,
A forum of fields, groves in a colonnade.

Nature is the same as Rome, and, it seems, once more
There is every reason for leaving the gods alone:
We have entrails after a sacrifice, to forecast war;
Slaves, to keep silence; and, for building, stone.   1914.

Пусть имена цветущих городов
Ласкают слух значительностью бренной.
Не город Рим живет среди веков,
А место человека во вселенной.

Им овладеть пытаются цари,
Священники оправдывают войны,
И без него презрения достойны,
Как жалкий сор, дома и алтари.

66.

Let the names of flowering cities
Caress the ear with their brief time of fame.
It's not Rome the city that lives through the centuries
But man's place in the universal scheme.

Kings try to capture that, and priests attempt
To use it when they justify a war;
Lacking that, houses and altars deserve contempt
Like a wretched heap of rubbish, nothing more.

Я не слыхал рассказов Оссиана,
Не пробовал старинного вина —
Зачем же мне мерещится поляна,
Шотландии кровавая луна?

И перекличка ворона и арфы
Мне чудится в зловещей тишине,
И ветром развеваемые шарфы
Дружинников мелькают при луне!

Я получил блаженное наследство —
Чужих певцов блуждающие сны;
Свое родство и скучное соседство
Мы презирать заведомо вольны.

И не одно сокровище, быть может,
Минуя внуков, к правнукам уйдет,
И снова скальд чужую песню сложит
И как свою ее произнесет.   1914.

I had never heard of Ossian's stories,
Had never tasted of that ancient wine—
Why does a glade appear before my eyes
Where the blood moon of Scotland shines?

I seem to hear, against a brooding silence,
Harp music mingled with a raven's croaks
And underneath the moon I catch a glimpse
Of clansmen slipping past in wind-tossed cloaks.

I have received a blessed legacy—
A foreign poet left me his wandering dreams;
And we can freely choose to think scornfully
How dull our kindred and surroundings seem.

And this may not be the only precious thing
That skips over grandsons, passing to their sons,
And a skald reshapes once more another's song
And sings it as his own.   1914.

68. ЕВРОПА

Как средиземный краб или звезда морская,
Был выброшен водой последний материк.
К широкой Азии, к Америке привык,
Слабеет океан, Европу омывая.

Изрезаны ее живые берега,
И полуостровов воздушны изваянья;
Немного женственны заливов очертанья:
Бискайи, Генуи ленивая дуга.

Завоевателей исконная земля,
Европа в рубище Священного Союза —
Пята Испании, Италии медуза
И Польша нежная, где нету короля.

Европа цезарей! С тех пор, как в Бонапарта
Гусиное перо направил Меттерних —
Впервые за сто лет и на глазах моих
Меняется твоя таинственная карта!   1914.

68. EUROPE

Like a crab or starfish from the Mediterranean,
The sea washed up this continent, last of them all.
Grown used to America, to vast Asia's sprawl,
Ocean licks at Europe and begins to weaken.

Her living coastlines have been carved away,
Peninsulas sculptured to fragility;
Outlines of bays are almost womanly,
The slackened bow of Genoa, Biscay.

A land for conquerors since time's beginning,
This Europe that Holy Alliance left rent and torn—
The Spanish heel, Italy's jellyfish form,
And gentle Poland, a kingdom with no king.

Europe of Caesars! since Metternich took aim
Pointing his goose-quill pen at Bonaparte—
Your mysterious map is changing before my eyes
After a century, for the first time.   1914.

69. ПОСОХ

Посох мой, моя свобода,
Сердцевина бытия —
Скоро ль истиной народа
Станет истина моя?

Я земле не поклонился
Прежде, чем себя нашел;
Посох взял, развеселился
И в далекий Рим пошел.

Пусть снега на черных пашнях
Не растают никогда,
Но печаль моих домашних
Мне попрежнему чужда.

Снег растает на утесах,
Солнцем истины палим.
Прав народ, вручивший посох
Мне, увидевшему Рим!   1914.

69. THE STAFF

My staff, my freedom,
My being's core—
Will the people's truth soon become
A truth I can share?

I studied my own heart
Before I bowed to the land;
Then I rejoiced to depart
For far Rome, with staff in hand.

Let the unmelting snow
Lie on black fields forever,
But the grief my people know
Is as foreign to me as ever.

Snow will melt on the cliff
In truth's blazing sun.
The people rightly gave the staff
To me, who has seen Rome.   1914.

70. 1 9 1 4

Собирались эллины войною
На прелестный остров Саламин, —
Он, отторгнут вражеской рукою,
Виден был из гавани Афин.

А теперь друзья-островитяне
Снаряжают наши корабли.
Не любили раньше англичане
Европейской сладостной земли.

О Европа, новая Эллада,
Охраняй Акрополь и Пирей!
Нам подарков с острова не надо —
Целый лес незваных кораблей.   1914.

70. 1914

The Greeks once mustered to make war
On Salamis, that charming island—
It was plainly visible from Athens' harbor,
Gripped by a hostile hand.

And now our island-dwelling friends
Are fitting out our ships of war.
The English have not loved the pleasant lands
Of Europe, not ever before.

O Europe, O new land of Hellas,
Guard the Acropolis, keep Piraeus fast!
We do not need the gifts the island gives us—
Unwelcome ships, an endless forest of masts.   [1916]

71. К ЭНЦИКЛИКЕ ПАПЫ БЕНЕДИКТА XV

Есть обитаемая духом
Свобода — избранных удел.
Орлиным зреньем, дивным слухом
Священник римский уцелел.

И голубь не боится грома,
Которым церковь говорит;
В апостольском созвучьи: Roma!
Он только сердце веселит.

Я повторяю это имя
Под вечным куполом небес,
Хоть говоривший мне о Риме
В священном сумраке исчез! 1914, сентябрь.

71. ON THE ENCYCLICAL OF POPE BENEDICT XV

There is a freedom dwelt in by the spirit,
The destiny that chosen souls attain.
With eagle eye, ears wonderfully alert,
The Roman priest has stayed sane.

The dove does not fear thundering
For thunder is the Church's voice;
Roma! the Apostolic music sings;
The heart can only rejoice.

I say this name again
Under heaven's everlasting dome
Though sacred gloom has swallowed up the man
Who spoke to me of Rome.   September 1914.

72. ОДА БЕТХОВЕНУ

Бывает сердце так сурово,
Что и любя его не тронь!
И в темной комнате глухого
Бетховена горит огонь.
И я не мог твоей, мучитель,
Чрезмерной радости понять..
Уже бросает исполнитель
Испепеленную тетрадь.

[Когда земля гудит от грома
И речка бурная ревет
Сильней грозы и бурелома,]
Кто этот дивный пешеход?
Он так стремительно ступает
С зеленой шляпою в руке,
[И ветер полы развевает
На неуклюжем сюртуке.]

С кем можно глубже и полнее
Всю чашу нежности испить,
Кто может ярче пламенея
Усилье воли освятить?
Кто по-крестьянски, сын фламандца,
Мир пригласил на ритурнель
И до тех пор не кончил танца,
Пока не вышел буйный хмель?

О Дионис, как муж наивный
И благодарный как дитя!
Ты перенес свой жребий дивный
То негодуя, то шутя!
С каким глухим негодованьем
Ты собирал с князей оброк

72. ODE TO BEETHOVEN

Sometimes there is a heart that is so stern
That though you love it, do not dare come near!
A darkened chamber where a fire burns,
Beethoven's chamber, he who cannot hear.
Tormentor, I could never come to know
The nature of your overflowing gladness.
And now already the performer throws
A page of score aside, burnt into ash.

[When earth itself is rumbling with thunder
And the river's turbulence is wildly howling
More violent than storms or winds that break the timber,]
Who is this amazing man out strolling?
He steps along with such impetuous spurts
Carrying in his hand his tall green hat,
[And the wind is fluttering the skirts
And lappets of his cumbersome frock coat.]

With whom can we drink more deeply from the cup
Of sentiment, and drain it to the lees?
Who can more ardently make flames blaze up
And more intensely sanctify liberty?
What man was it, what Flemish peasant's son
Who summoned all the world to join the dance
And would not say the *ritornelle* was done
Until it had drawn out all drunken violence?

O Dionysus, like a man who has no guile,
As full of gratitude as a child can be.
Sometimes indignant, sometimes with a smile,
Enduring your amazing destiny.
How much indignant pride did you repress
Picking up favors from your princely patrons,

Или с рассеянным вниманьем
На фортепьянный шел урок!

Тебе монашеские кельи —
Всемирной радости приют,
Тебе в пророческом весельи
Огнепоклонники поют;
Огонь пылает в человеке,
Его унять никто не мог.
Тебя назвать не смели греки,
Но чтили, неизвестный бог!

О величавой жертвы пламя!
Полнеба охватил костер —
И царской скинии над нами
Разодран шелковый шатер.
И в промежутке воспаленном,
Где мы не видим ничего, —
Ты указал в чертоге тронном
На белой славы торжество!   1914.

Or when, with absent-minded courtliness
You went to give the day's piano lesson!

A monk's cell is the place for you to be—
Where universal joy finds sheltering;
For you, in their prophetic gaiety,
The worshipers of fire sing;
Within mankind there burns a mighty flame,
A flame that no one ever could subdue.
The ancient Greeks feared to invoke your name
O unknown god, but still they honored you!

O flame of a majestic sacrifice!
Over half the sky the bonfire spreads—
Torn into rags, the silken tenting flies,
The holy shrine is ripped above our heads.
And in the open space amid the blaze
Where there is nothing at all that we can see—
You were in the throne room, and displayed
The triumph of a radiating glory!   1914.

Уничтожает пламень
Сухую жизнь мою,
И ныне я не камень,
А дерево пою.

Оно легко и грубо,
Из одного куска
И сердцевина дуба,
И весла рыбака.

Вбивайте крепче сваи,
Стучите, молотки,
О деревянном рае,
Где вещи так легки.   1914.

The fire tongues
My dry life away;
No more stone songs,
I sing wood today.

It is light and rough,
From one piece, no more;
Both the heart of the oak
And the fisherman's oar.

Drive piles more firmly in,
Hammers, pound tight,
O wooden heaven
Where all things are light.   1914.

74. АББАТ

О спутник вечного романа,
Аббат Флобера и Золя —
От зноя рыжая сутана
И шляпы круглые поля;
Он всё еще проходит мимо,
В тумане полдня, вдоль межи,
Влача остаток власти Рима
Среди колосьев спелой ржи.

Храня молчанье и приличье,
Он должен с нами пить и есть
И прятать в светское обличье
Сияющей тонзуры честь.
Он Цицерона, на перине,
Читает, отходя ко сну:
Так птицы на своей латыни
Молились Богу в старину.

Я поклонился, он ответил
Кивком учтивым головы,
И, говоря со мной, заметил:
«Католиком умрете вы!»
Потом вздохнул: «Как нынче жарко!»
И, разговором утомлен,
Направился к каштанам парка,
В тот замок, где обедал он.   1914.

74. THE ABBÉ

Our companion in the eternal *roman*,
Zola's *abbé*, the *abbé* of Flaubert—
Keeping the heat off with his rusty soutane
And the round-brimmed hat he wears;
Along the fields' borders, at the midday hour
Amid the floating haze, he passes by
Trailing one last remnant of Rome's power
Through the ripening ears of rye.

Silent, and decorous in his ways,
He has to eat and drink with us
And assumes a worldly manner, hiding away
His tonsure and its radiating nimbus.
When he lies down he reads in Cicero
On a feather bed, until he begins to nod:
So, in their own Latin, long ago
The birds once prayed to God.

And when we met I bowed to him, and he
Responded with a civil nod of the head,
And then, as he chatted there with me,
"You will die a Catholic," he said.
Later he sighed, "How hot it is today!"
And weary of too much talking, turned to go
Walking off toward the chestnuts in the park
On his way to dine at the château.   1914.

И поныне на Афоне
Древо чудное растет,
На крутом зеленом склоне
Имя Божие поет.

В каждой радуются келье
Имябожцы-мужики:
Слово — чистое веселье,
Исцеленье от тоски!

Всенародно, громогласно
Чернецы осуждены;
Но от ереси прекрасной
Мы спасаться не должны.

Каждый раз, когда мы любим,
Мы в нее впадаем вновь.
Безымянную мы губим
Вместе с именем любовь.   1915.

75.

And on Mount Athos even now
A tree miraculously springs
Upon the mountain's steep green brow
Where God's name sings.

Muzhiks rejoice in every cell,
The venerators of God's name:
The Word is total joy to them
And heals their pain.

Now all across the land we see
Monks facing public condemnation;
But from this lovely heresy
We need not seek salvation.

Every time we love anew
We lapse into heresy again.
We destroy nameless love
Together with love's name.   1915.

От вторника и до субботы
Одна пустыня пролегла.
О длительные перелеты!
Семь тысяч верст — одна стрела.

И ласточки, когда летели
В Египет водяным путем,
Четыре дня они висели,
Не зачерпнув воды крылом.   1915.

76.

From Tuesday until Saturday
The same waste desert lay below.
The flight was long—a single arrow,
The target seven thousand versts away.

And when the swallows made their flight,
Their overseas Egyptian journey,
For four days they hung aloft
And no wing scooped the sea.   1915.

77.

О свободе небывалой
Сладко думать у свечи.
— Ты побудь со мной сначала, —
Верность плакала в ночи.

— Только я мою корону
Возлагаю на тебя,
Чтоб свободе, как закону,
Подчинился ты, любя...

— Я свободе, как закону,
Обручен, и потому
Эту легкую корону
Никогда я не сниму.

Нам ли, брошенным в пространстве,
Обреченным умереть,
О прекрасном постоянстве
И о верности жалеть!   1915.

It is lovely to dream by candlelight
Of some fantastic liberty.
Loyalty was weeping in the night:
"Stay first awhile with me.

I place upon you my crown
And nothing more
So that loving, you may bow down
To liberty as to law . . . "

"To liberty as to law
I am betrothed
And so I will never take
This light crown off."

If we are abandoned in space
With death our destiny
Should we regret our faith
And our splendid constancy!   1915.

Бессонница. Гомер. Тугие паруса.
Я список кораблей прочел до середины:
Сей длинный выводок, сей поезд журавлиный,
Что над Элладою когда-то поднялся.

Как журавлиный клин в чужие рубежи —
На головах царей божественная пена —
Куда плывете вы? Когда бы не Елена,
Что Троя вам одна, ахейские мужи?

И море, и Гомер — всё движется любовью.
Кого же слушать мне? И вот Гомер молчит,
И море черное, витийствуя, шумит
И с тяжким грохотом подходит к изголовью.   1915.

Sleeplessness. Homer. The sails tight.
I have the catalogue of ships half read:
That file of cranes, long fledgling line that spread
And lifted once over Hellas, into flight.

Like a wedge of cranes into an alien place—
The god's spume foaming in the princes' hair—
Where do you sail? If Helen were not there
What would Troy matter, men of Achaean race?

The sea, and Homer—it's love that moves all things.
To whom should I listen? Homer falls silent now
And the black sea surges toward my pillow
Like a loud declaimer, heavily thundering.   1915.

79.

Обиженно уходят на холмы,
Как Римом недовольные плебеи,
Старухи-овцы — черные халдеи,
Исчадье ночи в капюшонах тьмы.

Их тысячи — передвигают все,
Как жердочки, мохнатые колени,
Трясутся и бегут в курчавой пене,
Как жеребья в огромном колесе.

Им нужен царь и черный Авентин,
Овечий Рим с его семью холмами,
Собачий лай, костер под небесами
И горький дым жилища и овин.

На них кустарник двинулся стеной,
И побежали воинов палатки,
Они идут в священном беспорядке.
Висит руно тяжелою волной.

Offended, they move off among the knolls
Like malcontent Roman plebians,
Old beldame ewes, black Chaldaeans,
Nighttime demons in their dark cowls.

There are thousands, all moving at once
On shaggy sticklike knees;
They tremble and run, in a foam of curly fleece
Like the balls in a huge wheel of chance.

It's their very own black Aventine they seek,
A seven-knolled ovine Rome, and their own tsar,
The barking of dogs, a fire in the open air,
Smoke from a shack or barn, with its bitter reek.

The bushes moved against them like a wall,
And then a sudden rush of warriors' tents;
They break away in sacred turbulence.
The fleece crests, a great wave poised to fall.

С веселым ржаниѐм пасутся табуны,
И римской ржавчиной окрасилась долина;
Сухое золото классической весны
Уносит времени прозрачная стремнина.

Топча по осени дубовые листы,
Что густо стелются пустынною тропинкой,
Я вспомню Цезаря прекрасные черты —
Сей профиль женственный с коварною горбинкой!

Здесь, Капитолия и Форума вдали,
Средь увядания спокойного природы,
Я слышу Августа и на краю земли
Державным яблоком катящиеся годы.

Да будет в старости печаль моя светла:
Я в Риме родился, и он ко мне вернулся;
Мне осень добрая волчицею была
И — месяц цезарей — мне август улыбнулся. 1915.

80.

Grazing horse herds joyfully neigh,
The valley has gone red with Roman rust;
Time's clear torrents are bearing away
A classical spring's gold dust.

Treading down oak leaves in fall
Thick on pathways where nobody goes
I will remember Caesar's perfect features—
Effeminate profile, crafty curving nose.

Here, amid the quiet fading of nature
Far from the Forum and the Capitol
I hear Augustus, and on the earth's rim I hear
The years rolling, like the sovereign apple.

When I am old, then let my sorrows shine:
I was born in Rome and Rome has come back to me;
The autumn was my she-wolf and was kind
And August—the month of Caesar—smiled on me.   1915.

Я не увижу знаменитой «Федры»,
В старинном многоярусном театре,
С прокопченной высокой галереи,
При свете оплывающих свечей.
И, равнодушен к суете актеров,
Сбирающих рукоплесканий жатву,
Я не услышу обращенный к рампе
Двойною рифмой опереный стих:

— Как эти покрывала мне постылы . . .

Театр Расина! Мощная завеса
Нас отделяет от другого мира;
Глубокими морщинами волнуя,
Меж ним и нами занавес лежит.
Спадают с плеч классические шали,
Расплавленный страданьем крепнет голос
И достигает скорбного закала
Негодованьем раскаленный слог . . .

Я опоздал на празднество Расина!

Вновь шелестят истлевшие афиши,
И слабо пахнет апельсинной коркой,
И словно из столетней летаргии —
Очнувшийся сосед мне говорит:
— Измученный безумством Мельпомены,
Я в этой жизни жажду только мира;
Уйдем, покуда зрители-шакалы
На растерзанье Музы не пришли!

Когда бы грек увидел наши игры . . .   1915.

I shall never see the famous *Phèdre*
In a many-galleried theater of long ago
Lighted by guttering candles
Where the highest tiers of seats are black with soot.
Indifferent to the preening of the actors
Gathering in their harvest of applause,
I shall not hear the verses cross the footlights,
Each of them feathered with a double rhyme:

—"These veils, how hateful they are to me . . . "

The theater of Racine! A heavy curtain
Closes us out of a different world;
In deadening and fluctuating folds
That curtain hangs between his world and ours.
Classical shawls are trailing down from shoulders,
A voice grows stronger, fused with suffering,
And the white-hot style, tempered with indignation,
Reaches an intensity of sorrow . . .

I came too late for the festival of Racine!

The decaying playbills rustle once again,
There is a faint odor of orange peel
And then, as if awakening from centuries
Of lethargy, a man beside me speaks:
"Melpomene's fury has exhausted me;
The only thing I want in life is peace.
Let us leave before an audience of jackals
Has gathered here to tear the Muse apart."

If a Greek were to see some play of ours . . .   1915.

NOTES

NOTES

The notes present: 1) the publication history of each poem before its inclusion in an edition of *Kamen'* (for the convenience of readers using Dymshitz's and Khardzhiev's *Stikhotvoreniia* [BP], I have added in parentheses the number used to refer to each poem in that edition); 2) the edition(s) of *Kamen'* in which each poem appears (since the four editions of *Kamen'* vary in contents and in the ordering of the poems, I have recorded the contents of each edition: each poem is listed by the number assigned to it by Struve and Filipoff, see pp. xi-xii); 3) variant or omitted lines and/or stanzas (these are all from SS and/or BP and so are not individually acknowledged); 4) explanations of references to persons, places, etc.; 5) suggested parallel passages in the works of other poets that Mandelstam may be quoting.

1(1). K2, K3, K4. Marina Cvetaeva, writing in *Ruski arhiv* [Russian archive] 26-27 (Belgrade, 1934): 115, suggests that stanza and pod fall together (B, p. 174).

2(2). K2 (stanza 1 only), K3, K4. BP compares line 6 to Tyutchev's "O my prophetic soul" ("O vyeshchaya dusha moya," 1855): "O my prophetic soul!/O heart, that is full of apprehension,/O how you contend together on the threshold/Of what seems a twofold life! . . . /Yes, you live in two worlds."

3(227). K2.

4(3). *Kovcheg* [The ark] (Feodosia, 1920). *Tristia*, 1922. K3, K4. Line 7: BP cites Fyodor Sologub, "I love my dark land." Another likely parallel is Tyutchev's "These poor villages" ("Eti bednye selen'ya," 1855): "These poor villages,/This barren nature—O long-suffering native land,/Land of the Russian people!"

5(4). K2, K3, K4.

6(5). *Al'manakhi stikhov, vikhodyashchie v Petrograde* [Almanacs of poems, published in Petrograd] Vol. 1, *Tsevnitsa* [The flute], 1915. K2, K3, K4. In K2, line 7 reads "Like the ones on an earthenware plate." Brown (B, pp. 168-169) comments on the lexical oddness of line 4, literally "It shyly vespered" or "It shyly evening-ed." The image of the artist drawing on porcelain or glass reappears in line 8. "Man ought to be the hardest thing of all on earth," Mandelstam wrote in "Concerning the Nature of the Word" ("O prirode slova"), "and ought to regard his relationship to the earth as that of a diamond to glass" (SS, 2: 300).

7(6). K2, K3, K4. Lyra: a constellation between Cygnus and Hercules, supposedly representing the lyre of Orpheus. Lares: the Lares and Penates were the household gods of the ancient Romans. Compare T. S. Eliot, "Burnt Norton": "Only by the form, the pattern,/Can words or music reach/The stillness, as a Chinese jar still/Moves perpetually in its stillness." Terras (p. 257) suggests a source in Southey's "Hymn to the Penates" (1796): "Yet not the less, PENATES, loved I then/Your altars; not the less at evening hour/ . . . by their fires/Tranquillity, in no unsocial mood,/Sits silent . . . /I will not quit,/ . . . your calm abodes." Pushkin translated Southey's "Hymn" in 1829.

8(7). *Apollon* [Apollo], no. 9 (August 1910). K1, K2, K3, K4. The publication of 13, 8, 147, 14, and 9 in *Apollon* (August 1910) constituted Mandelstam's literary debut. This is the first poem in K1, with the title "Breath" ("Dykhanie"); the title was dropped in subsequent editions. Brown says this is Mandelstam's most famous poem among Russian readers (B, p. 169), and comments on the unidiomatic "strangeness," especially in lines 1 and 5. The *Apollon* text has variants for line 1 (*"I have* a body" or *"possess* a body") and line 11 (*"While* the dregs of the moment seep away"). See also the note to poem 6. Mandelstam began his essay on Chaadaev by declaring, "The mark left by Chaadaev in the consciousness of Russian society is so deep and indelible that the question involuntarily arises: was it not done by a diamond on glass?" (SS, 2: 326).

9(8). *Apollon*, no. 9. K1, K2, K3, K4. In *Apollon*, line 11 reads, "And entrancingly alive." Mandelstam may be recalling Sully-Prudhomme's "Le vase brisé" (1865), well known in Russia in A. N. Apukhtin's translation (1870):

> The vase in which this vervaine is dying
> Was cracked by the blow of a fan;
> The blow must scarcely have grazed it.
> No noise made it known.
>
> But each day the gentle bruise
> Has been eating the crystal away
> With a certain and unseen progress
> And slowly made its way all around.

Day by day its fresh water has gone,
The flowers' nourishment drains away;
As yet no one suspects anything—
Touch it not, it is broken.

Often also the hand one loves
Grazing the heart, bruises it;
Then the heart itself breaks,
The flower of its love dies;

Still intact in the eyes of the world,
It weeps quietly
And feels its subtle deep wound grow—
It is broken—touch it not.

(Stances et poèmes, 1865)

10(24). *P'yanie vishni* [Drunken cherries], second edition (Sevastopol, 1920) (an anthology). K3, K4. Manuscript dated 16 November 1911. The weaving suggests the Parcae or Fates of Greek legend.

11(9). K2, K3, K4. Placed between 12 and 13 in K2 and K3. The manuscript is dated "Heidelberg, December 1909," and is arranged in six distichs, with the following distichs placed after the present second stanza:

For, if there is no meaning in life,
We should not talk about life.

I am still fairly wild at heart.
I am bored by our comprehensible
language.

The notion of a totality of existence not describable in words seems to look forward to "Silentium" (14). Terras (p. 255) recalls the Greek legends of dolphins, which were sacred to Apollo and friendly to man; a dolphin rescued the poet Arion and carried him to Sicily.

12(10). *Apollon*, no. 5 (May 1911). K2, K3, K4. All versions before K4 have a fourth stanza:

And the file retreats,
Shaking with laughter, and suddenly
Changed its mind and an arrow invites itself straight
into the heart,
Inscribing a circle as it goes.

In *Apollon*, the second line of this extra stanza read, "Shaking with springtime"; this was probably a misprint. The spindle may be that of the Parcae or Fates who weave the thread of a man's life (see *Odyssey* 7. 147), and a fear of savage arrows is a motif in Ovid's *Tristia* and *Epistulae ex Ponto* (see Terras, p. 257).

13(11). *Apollon*, no. 9. K1, K2, K3, K4. Mandelstam later compared the poets of ancient Greece to bees who produced "Ionic honey" (SS, poem 105); Taranovsky cites the poet-bee image from Plato's *Ion*, Horace, Ronsard, and Vyacheslav Ivanov (Taranovsky, pp. 86-87). The cold has silenced the hives and also the stream, another conventional metaphor for "natural" poetry (Duke Senior found "tongues in trees, books in the running brooks,/Sermons in stones . . ."). Taranovsky remarks on a parallel between stanza 3 and Andrey Bely's "Winter" ("Zima," 1907): "Let there be behind the wall, in the dim haze/Dry, dry, dry frost—/The gay swarm of diamond-like shimmering dragon-flies/Will fly on to the glass."

14(12). *Apollon*, no. 9. K1, K2, K3, K4. Untitled in *Apollon*. The title directs the reader (see Taranovsky, pp. 120-123) to Tyutchev's poem "Silentium!" (1830), a poem that suggests the futility of trying to communicate with any other human being, and advises living "within yourself": "A thought spoken is a lie;/Struggling, you stir up the waters,/Drink them, and keep silent." SS quotes Gumilyov's comment: "For the sake of the idea of music he [Mandelstam] is ready to forfeit the world." According to Terras (p. 257), Mandelstam knew Verlaine's phrase, "Music before everything else" ("*La musique avant toute chose*") from "Art poetique." Still a symbolist to some extent when he wrote this poem, he shared the Symbolist yearning for freedom from ordinary life and for an art "purer" than poetry; later, in "Someone Walking" (32), he seems to reply to "Silentium": "But from the abyss, music will not save me!" In "The Morning of Acmeism" ("Utro akmeizma"), he declares that "for Acmeists the overt meaning of a word, the Logos, is as glorious a form as music is for the Symbolists" (SS, 2: 363). Aphrodite is addressed just as she is about to be born of the sea-foam, in Greek *aphros* (B, p. 167). Since she is Love, she is that which creates and sustains all things: "love that moves all things" (78). Since she is not yet born, she is all procreating and (inevitably) separating activity *in potentia*; in her all opposites are as yet in unity. Brown (p. 166) suggests a comparison with "Seashell" (26) and with Botticelli's *Birth of Venus*.

Mandelstam's subsequent commitment to "the word as such" represents a repudiation of this poem's point of view, which interestingly anticipates that mistrust of the word which is such a central issue for twentieth-century philosophers (Wittgenstein) and writers (Samuel Beckett): "blot, words can be blotted and the mad thoughts they invent . . . all you have to do is say you said nothing and so say nothing again" (Beckett, "Texts for Nothing," *Stories and Texts for Nothing* [New York: Grove Press, 1967]).

15(13). *Severnye zapiski* [Northern notes], no. 9 (September 1913). K2, K3, K4. In *Severnye zapiski*, the poem began with a stanza subsequently discarded: "The soul is weary from her efforts,/And it is all the same to me./Whiter than lilies, the white night/Looks fearfully in at the window"; then stanza 2 began with "The keen ear is a sail stretched taut." In K2, only the last two stanzas appeared, beginning "I am as poor as nature." BP compares line 7, "My freedom is as spectral," to Tyutchev, "It is only in our faint freedom," from his "There is a melody in the waves of the sea" ("Pyevuchest' yest' v morskikh volnakh," 1865); and line 11, "Though your world is morbid and alien," to his "Your day is morbid and passionate" from "O my prophetic soul!" ("O vyeshchaya dusha moya"; 1855). In *Mozart and Salieri* (trans. Robert A. McLean [Ann Arbor: Ardis, 1973], p. 41), Nadezhda Mandelstam says that at a conference on the psychology of writing poetry, a speaker used this poem to describe the poet's moment of special quiet and attentive listening, waiting for the poem to "come."

16(14). *Apollon*, no. 5. K4. In *Apollon*, there was a full third stanza: "In the breakers a boat is rustling/Like foliage—far away already/And taking the wind of doom,/My soul opened its sail."

17(15). *Apollon*, no. 5. K4. The *Apollon* version has a fourth stanza: "I do not experience sweetness in torment/Nor do I look for meaning in it;/With the final victory at hand,/perhaps I will have revenge for everything." Taranovsky (pp. 51-54) invokes Omry Ronen's theory that in this poem and in poem 18 the pond and the mud represent the "Judaic chaos" that Mandelstam wanted to escape; Taranovsky also suggests that the "rustling reed" image comes from

Tyutchev's "Pyevuchest' yest' " (see note to poem 15): "And a harmonious musical rustling/Runs through the tossing reeds." He cites Mandelstam's reference to Tyutchev's poem in his essay "Pushkin and Scriabin": "Something has happened to music, some kind of wind has broken the dry clear musical reeds with a sudden gust. We require a chorus, the murmuring of the thinking reed bores us" (SS, 2: 359). The "thinking reed" is Pascal's *roseau pensant*: "Man is no more than a reed, the weakest thing in nature; but he is a thinking reed" ("L'homme n'est qu'un roseau, le plus faible de la nature; mais c'est un roseau pensant"; *Pensées* 6.347). The reed, a potential source of music, is a metaphor for the poet: Mandelstam is presumably drawing on the epigraph to Tyutchev's poem, a line from Ausonius's *epistulae* (25.13): "Est in arundineis modulatio musica ripis" [There is musical melody in the reeds along the bank]. Is there a submerged pun operating between *kamish*, reed, and *kamen'*, stone? They are, in a sense, juxtaposed in "Notre Dame" (39).

18(16). *Apollon*, no. 5. K2, K3, K4.

19(234). K2.

20(17). K2, K3, K4. Brown (pp. 231-233) comments on the importance of Pushkin's secret burial by night, in January, for some of Mandelstam's later poems and images; the event may also underlie this poem.

21(18). *Literaturnii al'manakh*, 1912 [Literary almanac], published by *Apollon*, which appeared in November 1911. K1, K2, K3, K4. The silent tower suggests a reference to Vyacheslav Ivanov and his "Tower" (*Bashnya*), the St. Petersburg apartment where poets met weekly to read and discuss their work. Mandelstam uses *kolokol'ni*, bell tower, in line 7, but shifts to *bashnya* in line 11. The appearance of the poem coincided with Gumilyov's founding of the Poets' Workshop in November 1911, the beginning of the Acmeist movement. Ivanov left the Tower and went abroad early in 1912. In a 1924 essay, "A Thrust" ("Vypad"), Mandelstam refers to "the tolling bells of Vyacheslav Ivanov" (SS, 2: 272).

22(19). K2, K3, K4. In 1936, during his Voronezh exile, Mandelstam altered line 8 to "Where (I am) alone in single solitude." The poem's references to a shot and some national shame suggest to me a connection with the assassination of

Stolypin, the Russian prime minister, shot in a Kiev theater on 14 September 1911 by a Jew, Mordka Bogrov. Stolypin's death was one in a long series of political assassinations and attempted assassinations going back to the reign of Alexander II (1855-1881). These assassinations (Stolypin's especially) were followed by savage pogroms in Jewish areas. Mandelstam may be recalling the second stanza of Tyutchev's "So he is saved! It could not have been otherwise!" ("Tak! On spasen! Inache byt' ne mozhet!"), written on 4 April 1866, the day Alexander II narrowly escaped assassination: "Everything in us, everything is shamed by this shot,/And the outrage will not go away:/It lies, alas, it lies as a shameful blemish/On the whole history of the Russian people!"

23(20). *Giperborei* [The Hyperborean], no. 1 (October 1912). K1, K2, K3, K4. According to Lily Brik (SS), this poem "delighted" Mayakovsky. Line 2 echoes Pushkin, *Eugene Onegin* 7.15: "The beetle churred./The choral throngs already were dispersing" (trans. Vladimir Nabokov, [Princeton University Press, 1975]).

24(21). K1, K2, K3, K4.

25(22). *Giperborei*, no. 1. K1, K2, K3, K4. Through K2, line 10 reads, "You went into the realms of the sea." Aquilon: the North Wind. Orphic: the poet Orpheus went with the Argonauts to seek the Golden Fleece. His poems could move material objects and at the same time were mystical hymns that penetrated the secrets of the universe, a fact that made him of great interest to the Symbolists. He was supposedly the son of Apollo and was torn to pieces by the Maenad worshippers of Dionysus, after which his singing head floated across the sea to Lesbos. He is the traditional founder of Orphism, a mystical cult that included among its doctrines the notion that the body and the material world imprison the soul. Nadezhda Mandelstam sees both Aquilon and the Orphic wind as metaphors for the divine afflatus, the poet's sudden moment of inspiration (*Mozart and Salieri*, pp. 45-48). The relinquished "I," which implies an abandoning of the individual personality, restates a Symbolist idea probably derived from Pascal's "The 'I' is hateful" ("Le *moi* est haissable," *Pensées* 7. 455). Mandelstam learned that the last two lines of this poem had been scratched on the wall of a death cell in one of Stalin's concentration camps (N. Mandelstam, *Hope Against Hope*, trans. Max Hayward [New York: Athenaeum, 1976], p. 381).

26(23). K1, K2, K3, K4. Untitled in K1. Brown (p. 162) points out the use of one of Pushkin's favorite meters and the quotation from *Eugene Onegin* ("the house of a heart not lived in"); Pushkin uses the image in 6.32 to describe the dead Lensky just after the duel: "One moment earlier/in *this* heart had throbbed inspiration,/ . . . now, as in a deserted house,/all in it is both still and dark,/it has become forever silent" (trans. Vladimir Nabokov [Princeton: Princeton University Press, 1975]). A shell provides a way for the "natural" poetry in the universe to be heard (B, p. 162). Taranovsky (p. 79) describes night as "the creative force which fills the shell (that is, the poet) with impressions of the outer world" and refers (p. 142, note 10) to Gumilyov's "The Discovery of America" ("Otkrytie Ameriki," 1910): "I am a shell, but a shell without pearls,/I am a torrent which has been dammed—/Let free, but still not needed." Brown (p. 161) says that Mandelstam initially planned to call his first book "Seashell" ("Rakovina") rather than *Stone*.

27(25). *Severnye zapiski*, no. 9. K2, K3, K4. Manuscript dated 24 November 1911. In the *Severnye zapiski* version there are four stanzas:

The wind shakes the slender twigs,
And the voice of the copper wires grows strong,
And blazing tatters are staining the snow—
All that's left from a poor notebook.

Oh sky, sky, I'm going to dream about you!
It can't be that you've gone completely blind,
That the day, like a sheet of blank paper, has burnt through
Leaving only a little smoke and ash behind!

Pearly handwriting showed deceptively,
And the lace did not really need to form a pattern,
And only the copper—invincibly quivering—
Cuts space, threading it with black glass.

Do I perhaps know why I am weeping?
I can only sing and die.
Do not trouble me: I do not mean anything
And I cherish black chaos in black dreams.

Mandelstam may be thinking of an 1830 poem by Tyutchev, "As on the fiery embers" ("Kak nad goryacheyo zoloi"):

> Just as a scroll smoulders and burns
>   through
> Upon the fiery embers,
> And hidden and secret, the fire
> Devours the words and lines:
>
> So my life smoulders sadly
> And each day goes up in smoke;
> So I vanish, moment by moment,
> Into unbearable monotony! . . .
>
> Oh sky, I wish that just once
> My fire would blaze up freely,
> And, no longer in pain and torment,
> I could flare up—and go out!

28(26). *Giperborei*, no. 1. K2, K3, K4. In 1937, in Voronezh, Mandelstam cancelled stanza 4 in his copy of K4 and replaced it with

> What if, quivering irregularly,
> Where it twinkles eternally,
> A star with its rusty pin
> Should reach me?

Line 2 can also be translated "I want to become mute" (*one-met'* can mean either *dumb* or *numb*).

29(27). K1, K2, K3, K4. A copy in Mandelstam's handwriting has lines 5-6 as "Stone, become an avenger,/Stand with your pointed lace." The "Tower that thins to an arrow of spire" probably refers to the spire on the Admiralty in St. Petersburg (see note to poem 48). "For Mandelstam the sky has never been the dwelling place of God, because he felt too clearly His existence outside of space and time. . . . The task of man is to bring life to [the empty heavens] by making them commensurate with the work of his hands—a cupola, a tower, a gothic arch" (N. Mandelstam, *Mozart and Salieri*, p. 67). In *The Egyptian Stamp*, Mandelstam speaks of "the delirium of the Petersburg influenza . . . my dear prosaic delirium," a state in which solid objects like barriers, buildings, and pianos seem to be in a state of constant agitation. "To build means to contend with the void, to hypnotize space," he says in "The Morning of Acmeism" (1913). "The beautiful shaft of the Gothic belltower is angry, for the entire meaning of it is to stab the sky, to reproach it because it is empty" (SS, 2:365). Discussing Chaadaev's enforced silence, Mandelstam asks, "Had his Gothic thought submitted and ceased to raise its arrow-like tower into the sky?" (SS, 2:329).

30(28). *Giperborei*, no. 1. K1, K2, K3, K4. A fair copy is dated April 1912. The image of God's name having its own separate identity, existence, and will may obliquely refer to the teaching of the *Imyabozhtsi* or "God's Name" movement (see note to poem 75).

31(29). K1, K2, K3, K4. Konstantin Batyushkov (1787-1855) wrote rather sensual poetry in a neoclassical style. He tried to make Russian writers more aware of the culture of the Mediterranean world, and he translated the *Greek Anthology* into Russian. He became permanently insane in 1821, thereafter writing nothing. The reply recorded in the poem was given during his long confinement in an asylum.

In a note to his "The Old Clock on the Stairs," Longfellow attributes a similar anecdote to the French preacher Jacques Bridaine (1701-1767): " . . . un réprouvé s'écrie, 'Quelle heure est-il?' et la voix d'un autre misérable lui répond, 'L'Eternité' " [one of the condemned cries out, "What time is it?" and the voice of another wretch replies, "Eternity"].

Reviewing the 1913 and later the 1916 *Kamen'* for *Apollon*, Gumilyov pointed to Poem 31 as the moment of Mandelstam's conversion to Acmeist principles (Gumilyov, 4:326-328; 363-366). Mandelstam commended François Villon for not yearning, as the Symbolists did, for the unattainable, especially for the unattainable moon (B, pp. 178-179): "The moon and other neutral 'objects' are kept irrevocably out of [Villon's] poetic vocabulary. But on the other hand, he revives immediately when the discussion arrives at roast ducks with gravy or at everlasting bliss—things he never loses a definite hope of obtaining" ("François Villon," SS, 2: 348).

32(30). K1, K2, K3, K4. In K2, this poem was dedicated to Mikhail Lozinsky, poet, translator, and editor of *Giperborei*; untitled in K3. Brown (p. 180) suggests that this poem is a "reply" to Poem 31, and perhaps also to a poem by Andrey Bely, "The Meeting" ("Vstrecha") (B, p. 307, n. 7); I think

that it also replies to Mandelstam's own "Silentium" (14).
To the Symbolists, Verlaine's phrase, "La musique avant
toute chose," was a popular slogan, and they were fasci-
nated by chasms, precipices, abysses. Taranovsky (p. 17) re-
marks that the last line repudiates Scriabin's belief that
music can save mankind. Mandelstam sees both the swal-
low and the stone tower as soaring.

33(31). *Giperborei*, no. 3 (December 1912). K1, K2, K3, K4. A fair
copy is dated May 1912. See my comparison (Introduction,
pp. 21-23) of this poem and Blok's "In the Restaurant" (pub-
lished November 1911). Blok's lines 7-8, "I sent you a black
rose in a glass/Of Aï that was as gold as the sky" (Aï is a
brand of champagne), seem to be echoed in Mandelstam's
line 13. In *The Sound of Time (Shum Vremeni)*, he de-
scribes family holidays at Dubbeln, near Riga on the Lat-
vian coast (P, pp. 88-94), probably the locale of this poem.
Taranovsky (p. 159, n. 18) points out a quotation from Afa-
nasy Fet's "Swallows" ("Lastochki," 1884): "Forgetting
everything around me, I love/To look at arrowlike swal-
lows."

34(244). *Giperborei*, no. 8 (October 1913). K2. The falling stones
in stanza 1 suggest Tyutchev's "stone that rolled down off
the mountain, . . . How did it fall? No one knows now—/Did
it break away . . . *by itself,*/Or [was it] hurled down by some
deliberate hand?", a passage that gave *Kamen'* its name (see
Introduction). In *The Sound of Time*, Mandelstam calls the
"civic poet" Semyon Nadson (1862-1887) "this wooden
monk" (P, p. 84; see also Introduction). The essay "Human-
ism and Contemporary Life" ("Gumanizm i sovremen-
nost'," 1923) offers a kind of commentary on the final lines:

> Repudiate social architecture [i.e., a harmonious and
> fair relationship between the parts of the body politic]
> and you destroy the simplest, the most universally ac-
> cepted, and the most neccessary structure—you de-
> stroy man's house, the human dwelling.
>
> In countries where earthquakes are a danger, the peo-
> ple build close to the ground and this inclination to-
> ward flatness, beginning with the French Revolution,
> pervades the entire legal life of the nineteenth century,
> all of which passed in a state of tensely awaiting some
> underground tremor, some social shock. . . .
>
> How are we to protect the human dwelling against

the terrible shocks, where are we to shore up its walls against the subterranean tremors of history? (SS, 2: 395).

The oppressive atmosphere of a Gothic cloister is characteristic of Gothic novels like *The Monk* and *Melmoth the Wanderer* and of some of Poe's tales.

35(245). K1, K2. Mandelstam intended to include the poem in K4. The wartime censor who passed K2 insisted that Mandelstam substitute *zealously (r'yani)* for *drunkenly (p'yani)* in line 2. BP gives stanza 1 as follows:

> Let's go to Tsarskoe Selo!
> Petty bourgeois are smiling there,
> When the hussars, after drinking,
> Sit firmly in the saddle . . .
> Let's go to Tsarskoe Selo!

The source for this variant is not identified.

Mandelstam calls the lancers *ulani*, Uhlans, a detail that caused Akhmatova to accuse him of "emphatic carelessness. . . . There were never Uhlans in Tsarskoe, but there were Hussars, Yellow Cuirassiers, and escort troops" ("Mandelstam," AAS, 2: 177). There were certainly Uhlan regiments in the imperial Russian army: Gumilyov joined the Uhlan regiment of the (imperial) Bodyguard when World War I broke out.

Tsarskoe Selo (Tsar's Village; Imperial village), now Pushkin (Pushkin attended school there), is about fifteen miles south of St. Petersburg/Leningrad, contains several imperial palaces, and was a residence for the court during part of each year. The town was a favorite place of retirement for soldiers and officials. In *The Sound of Time*, Mandelstam describes his family's life in another palace suburb, Pavlovsk, a few miles away:

> . . . that old ladies' town, that Russian demi-Versailles, the city of court lackeys, widows of high officials, red-headed policemen, consumptive pedagogues . . . and grafters who had raked together enough money for a detached villa. . . . When carefully bound volumes of *The Field* . . . were to constitute for a long time to come the basis of the libraries of the petty bourgeoisie. (P, p. 70)

Niva [The field] was a popular literary magazine, published from 1870 to 1918; novels by Turgenev, Tolstoy, and Leskov appeared in "bonus" editions for its subscribers.

Georgy Vladimirovich Ivanov (1894-1958), a minor member of the Acmeist group, emigrated to Paris after the Revolution; he wrote a very fanciful account of a nocturnal journey to Tsarskoe Selo with Mandelstam, Gumilyov, and Akhmatova in what Akhmatova called "his penny dreadful memoirs," *Peterburgskie zimi* [Petersburg winters, 1928]; see B, pp. 14-16; "Mandelstam," AAS, 2: 186.

36(32). K1, K2, K3, K4. The speaker has either a five- or a ten-ruble gold piece, the only gold coins current in Russia at the time. "The transition to gold currency is the business of the future," Mandelstam writes in "Humanism and the Present" (1923), "and we shall see the replacement of temporary ideas—paper notes—by the gold coinage of the European humanistic tradition, and the splendid florins of humanism will ring not against the archaeologist's spade but in the light of their own day and, when the moment has come, will be the hard cash that passes from hand to hand" (translated by B, p. 104; SS, 2: 396).

37(33). *Giperborei*, no. 5 (February 1913). K1, K2, K3, K4. Untitled in *Giperborei*. In *The Sound of Time*, Mandelstam mentions "Elderly German women" at a funeral in St. Petersburg, "their cheeks glowing and their mourning freshly donned" (P, p. 93). Line 22 is a reference to St. John the Baptist, who described himself as not the Savior but one sent to announce that the Savior was at hand; his cry was "Prepare ye the way of the Lord" (Mark 1:3; Luke 3:4). Mandelstam's poem evokes two poems by Tyutchev, "I love the Lutheran order of worship" ("Ya lyuteran lyublyu bogosluzhen'e," 1834) and "The coffin is lowered into the grave" ("I grob opushchen uzh v mogilu," 1836):

> I love the Lutheran order of worship,
> Their austere ritual, solemn and plain—
> I understand the lofty teaching
> Of these bare walls, this empty temple.
>
> Don't you see? Ready for the road,
> Faith is among you for the last time:
> She has not yet crossed the threshold,
> But already the house stands empty and bare . . .

"The coffin is lowered into the grave" contains the lines, "A dignified and learned pastor/Pronounces a funeral oration . . . /" and "The sensible and decorous oration/Holds the diverse crowd's attention." SS cites both parallels.

38(34). *Apollon*, no. 3 (March 1913). K1, K2, K3, K4. K1 and K2 have "And Justinian's years are a model to all" (1. 5) and "To what did your lavish architect aspire?" (1. 9). The Byzantine Emperor Justinian (527-565) built the great church of Hagia Sophia in Constantinople (Istanbul); it is not dedicated to a saint but to the concept of Holy or Divine Wisdom (Sophia). For Vladimir Solovyov and the mystical Symbolists, Sophia was an enigmatic and elusive feminine figure, occasionally glimpsed and always sought; for Mandelstam—and Justinian—Sophia is a real stone church. The temple of Diana at Ephesus was one of the seven wonders of the ancient world. "Many temples of the old religion contributed to the construction of the Church of the Divine Wisdom; and the edifice of Sophia was supported on the columns of Isis and Osiris, on the pillars of the Temples of the Sun and Moon at Heliopolis and Ephesus" *Murray's Handbook for Travellers in Constantinople, Brûsa, and the Troad* (London, 1900), p. 46. Exedrae are semicircular side-chapels; pendentives (Russian *parusi*, literally *sails*) are the triangular curved surfaces created by the intersection of the four great arches supporting the central dome; each contains a picture of a six-winged seraph.

Brown (p. 187) points out that in both this poem and in Poem 39, "Notre Dame," the words *sudil* (made or framed a law) and *narod* (nation, folk) occur in stanza 1, a further link between the two poems, which were originally published together.

39(35). *Apollon*, no. 3. K1, K2, K3, K4. A fair copy offers as stanza 1:

> The alluring flight of the traceried galleries—
> And, with tendons stretched and nerves straining,
> Like Adam long ago, mysterious and new born,
> The light cross-vaulting is flexing every muscle.

The Roman judge recalls the origin of Paris as a Roman colony. There is a statue of Adam on the façade of Notre Dame; Mandelstam is also probably thinking of Michelangelo's Adam on the ceiling of the Sistine Chapel and of the fact that the Acmeists sometimes called themselves Adamists. Sergey Gorodetsky's poem "Adam" appeared in *Apollon* a few pages before "Notre Dame." The "thin reed" of line 12, and the poem's interest in architectural measurement, recalls Rev. 11:1: "And there was given me a reed like unto a rod: and the angel stood, saying, Rise, and measure the temple of God."

BP cites a passage from "The Morning of Acmeism": "Acmeists share an enthusiasm for the organism and for organization with the Middle Ages, an era of physiological genius. . . . Notre Dame is a celebration of physiology, its Dionysian revelry" (SS, 2: 365). See also "Humanism and Contemporary Life," which defines "social Gothic" as "the free play of mass and force, human society conceived as a complex and thick architectural forest, where everything is fitting and each individual detail speaks in harmony with the vast totality" (SS, 2: 395). Mandelstam compares Gothic cathedrals to forests in "Concerning the Nature of the Word" (SS, 2: 292-293).

40(36). *Giperborei*, no. 9-10 (November-December 1913). K2, K3, K4. A manuscript fair copy is dated 1912. In printed versions through K4, the last line reads "I don't have a scarf to wrap around my throat"; Mandelstam changed the text to the present version by a note in his copy of K4, dated "Voronezh, 2 January 1937." Poe became popular in Russia after about 1900, in translations by Balmont, Bryusov, and others. One of Poe's translators, Vladimir Pyast (1886-1940), was subject to nervous seizures that left him unable to speak; Mandelstam was present on one such occasion, when Pyast was reading his translations in public but broke down and stared silently at the audience until everyone left the hall (B, p. 200). In "Storm and Stress" ("Burya i natisk") Mandelstam praises Balmont for "phonetic brilliance" and adds that he "elicits from Russian verse new sounds which could not be repeated again, sounds of an alien, somehow of a seraphic phonetic" (SS, 2: 384). Mandelstam seems to be suggesting that in Poe sound is more important than sense. Mandelstam thought that Poe—at any rate, in Balmont's versions—would have little effect on Russian poetry (SS, 2: 293).

41(37). K1, K2, K3, K4. In K1, K2, and K3, line 20 reads "Gay needs." In 1937, during his Voronezh exile, Mandelstam cancelled all of stanza 5. The protagonist may owe something to Rasputin, who was already notorious when it was written. Rasputin called himself *starets*, elder, a title unofficially given to monks who undertook the spiritual guidance of disciples, and the poem's title, *starik* (old man), echoes this. Rasputin's drunkenness and lechery were well known, and he adopted the maxim, "Sin in order that you may obtain forgiveness," an idea that stanza 3 seems to reflect.

42(38). *Giperborei*, no. 5. K1, K2, K3, K4. No dedication in *Giperborei*. Manuscript dated January 1913. In K1 and K2, line 11 reads, "And the strong purple of the state." In K1 there are three dots after the last word of stanza 4, and in K2 a row of dots between stanzas 4 and 5. Lily Brik (BP) listed this poem among those that Mayakovsky knew by heart. The "law student" (*pravoved*) of line 11 attends a special law school on the Fontanka Canal that was open only to young men of noble family (see Baedeker's *Russia*, 1914 edition, p. 126). Mandelstam's poem recalls a number of real or fictional episodes in the history of St. Petersburg. He refers to poems and stories that are partly or entirely set in the city: Gogol's "The Overcoat" (1. 4), and Pushkin's *Eugene Onegin* (the "northern snob" of line 13) and *The Bronze Horseman* ("Queer proud Evgeni" is the hero of that poem). The yellow stone of the buildings suggests the emperors (the imperial standard was yellow and black), as does the purple of line 11. The Admiralty, on the Neva quays, is at the heart of the city and stands for its most important role: a "window on the West" through which Western culture can enter Russia. The Senate Square, with its snow and bayonet, recalls the suppression of the Decembrist revolt there in 1825. The ice-bound ships (ll. 5-6) echo Ovid's *Tristia* (3. 10.47-48): "inclusaeque gelu stabunt in marmore puppes,/ nec poterit rigidas findere remus aquas" [The ships, shut in by the cold, stand in the marble, and the oar cannot cut through the hardened waters].

Pushkin's *Bronze Horseman* underlies Mandelstam's poem and is quoted or referred to in line 9 ("half the globe," *Bronze Horseman*, 1. 427), line 11 (Pushkin's references to imperial purple in BH, 11. 41-42; 332), and probably in line 15, which introduces the Bronze Horseman himself, Falconet's equestrian statue of Peter the Great (1782) mounted on a 1500 ton "wave" of granite in the middle of Senate Square, and the flood that fills that Square in Pushkin's poem.

43(39). K4. The German phrase, translated in the first line, is from Martin Luther's speech explaining and defending his principles before Charles V at the Diet of Worms in April 1521.

44(252). *Al'manakh muz* [Almanac of the Muses], 1916. *Tristia*, 1922; assigned to *Stone* by Struve and Filipoff. A manuscript text for stanza 1 reads:

> We went insane from living indulgently.
> Grown gray from reckless gaiety—
> It is time, time to stop the swings
> While darkness does not yet prevail entirely.

"That fellow there" is probably Georgy Ivanov (B, p. 199); see note to poem 37. The poem is dated 10 November 1913 in the manuscript, and is a kind of commentary (BP) on a poem Akhmatova wrote in January 1913 about the Bohemian nightclub "The Stray Dog," which was frequented by writers and artists:

> Cabaret artistique
> We are all revelers here, whores,
> And how sad we are together!
> The flowers and birds on the walls
> Yearn for clouds.
>
> You smoke a blackened pipe,
> With such strange clouds of smoke above
>   you.
> I have put on a tight skirt
> To show that I am slim still.
>
> . . . .
>
> O how heavy my heart is!
> Am I not awaiting the hour of death?
> But that one, who is dancing now,
> Will surely be in hell.
>
> (AAS, 1: 97)

BP suggests that the "drunken plague" is connected with Pushkin's miniature tragedy, *Pir vo vremya chumi* [The feast in a time of plague; 1830], adapted from a scene in John Wilson's *The City of the Plague* (1816).

45(40). *Giperborei*, no. 5. K1, K2, K3, K4. In *Giperborei* and K1, there is an additional stanza at the beginning of the poem:

> A foreigner in a stuffy bar,
> I often, at a late hour,

> Leaving the stupified drunkards,
> Find myself.

For the Bronze Horseman (1.8), see note to Poem 42. The fort is Petropavlovsk (St. Peter and Paul) Fortress across the Neva from the Winter Palace. A cannon was fired from the fortress to warn the inhabitants of St. Petersburg of spring-time floods; poor people who lived in cellars (see Dostoevsky's *Notes from Underground*) were especially vulnerable, and "poor Evgeni's" sufferings during such a flood form the central events of Pushkin's *Bronze Horseman*.

46(41). *Giperborei*, no. 9-10. K2, K3, K4. Mandelstam echoes Tyutchev's "I love the Lutheran order of worship" (see note to Poem 37). Isaiah: Bach's chorale "Isaiah, rejoice," was often played at Lutheran weddings (BP). Mandelstam admired Bach as a hard-working and meticulous craftsman rather than as an "inspired" composer; *Mozart and Salieri* records his preference for the hard-working Salieri over the genius Mozart. See also "The Morning of Acmeism":

> We have come to love the music of proving. . . . How convincing Bach's music is! What a power of proving! We must prove and prove without ceasing: to accept anything on faith in art is not worthy of an artist, it is lazy and boring. . . . We do not fly, we only climb up those towers that we can construct ourselves. (SS, 2: 366-367; cited in BP)

47(42). *Rubicon*, no. 3 (14 February 1914). K2, K3, K4. As published in *Rubicon*, the poem had a title, "The Tea-Room." *Muzhik* is a slightly condescending term for a peasant.

48(43). *Apollon*, no. 10 (December 1914). K2, K3, K4. A fair copy is dated May 1913; in it, stanza 4 precedes stanza 3, and there is a fifth stanza:

> The living avenue shifts, like a swan.
> I converse once more with the Muse of architecture.
> The sightlines grow clear, life's tremors grow still—
> It is all the same to me, wherever and whenever I exist.

The Admiralty, designed by A. Zakharov in 1806, stands beside the Neva, and the three main avenues of St. Petersburg radiate from its square. Brown (p. 307, n. 11) points out that *lad'ia*, "ship" (1. 5), can also mean a rook in chess, which has power down long vistas of the chessboard. The Admiralty is organized around a large central arch surmounted by a kind of Ionic temple from which rises a tall slender golden spire with a weather vane in the shape of a ship on top. In *Voyage en Russie* (1866) Théophile Gautier described it as "the mast of a golden ship planted on the roof of a Greek temple." The medusae are both real jellyfish and the carved stone faces on various Petersburg buildings. "In order to build successfully, the first condition is sincere reverence toward the three dimensions of space," Mandelstam writes in "The Morning of Acmeism," "to look on them not as a burden and an unfortunate accident but as a palace which is a gift of God" (SS, 2: 364). It is important to remember that Peter the Great was trained as a carpenter.

49(44). *Giperborei*, no. 8. K2, K3, K4. There is a fair copy with a title, "The Tavern." The tower in line 5 may be a sardonic reference to Vyacheslav Ivanov's gatherings of poets. Mandelstam portrays the preacher as a kind of carnival barker, making his pitch to attract a crowd. The sand suggests eternity because sand is used in hourglasses; in *The Sound of Time*, Mandelstam mentioned the "oozy, pure yellow, and astonishingly fine sand (even in an hourglass one could hardly find such sand!)" of the district around Riga (P, p. 92); this poem's setting may be Riga's medieval "Old Town," some recollected Italian scene, or even an opera. Konstantin Balmont ends his "An Appeal to the Ocean" ("Vozzvan'e k okeanu," ca. 1900) with the lines, "Let me be a wet speck of your sand,/A grain in the eternal . . . Eternity! Ocean!"

50(45). *Novii Satirikon* [The new satyricon], no. 22 (1914). K2, K3, K4.

51(46). *Za 7 dnei* [During seven days], no. 20 (20 June 1913); *Novii Satirikon*, no. 24 (1914). K2, K3, K4. When the poem appeared in *Za 7 dnei*, it did not include stanza 3; stanzas 1, 2, and 4 were followed by three additional stanzas:

> I see mills, as in the old days,
> And rowers on the gentle Thames;
> A shy sportsman took possession
> Of a very merry boat.

> I see a flock at the water;
> Sheep dogs are watching the sheep.
> Free of saddle and bridle,
> A horse is let into the bright clover.

This is England in flower—
A peaceful merry island . . .
Hail to you, tennis flight,
Linen, and a bare arm.

Tennis, or lawn tennis, was invented in 1874 by an English-
man, Major Wingfield, who called it *"Sphairistike* or Lawn
Tennis"; this information was available to Mandelstam in
the Brockhaus *Entsiklopedia Slovar'*. The game was
quickly introduced into Russia (tennis is among the amen-
ities of Vronsky's estate in *Anna Karenina*). The "Lilacs
reeking of gasoline" (l. 20) echo Akhmatova's "A smell of
gasoline and lilacs" in her "A Stroll" ("Progulka"), written in
May 1913 (BP; see also AAS, 1: 100). Mayakovsky once
greeted Mandelstam by shouting lines 15-16 at him (B, p.
100).

52(47). *P'yanie vishni*. K3, K4. There is a corrected galley proof
from no. 9 (not published) of the journal *Rudin* (1916). The
Titanic sank on 15 April 1912. Okeanos and his light-footed
daughters, the Okeanids (Oceanids), visit the Caucasus in
Prometheus Bound. Odysseus, addressing Nausikaa (*Odys-
sey* 6: 160-170), compares her to "the trunk of a young palm
shooting up," which he had once seen "in Delos . . . by
Apollo's altar." Mandelstam's cluster of Greek temples, the
shipwreck, and a maiden compared to a tree seems to in-
voke this. King Louis is a mixture of Louis XIV, XV, XVI;
the girl would be vague about their dates and deeds.

53(49). *Novii Satirikon*, no. 7 (13 February 1914). K2, K3, K4. See
Introduction, pp. 35-36. "One summer afternoon . . . there
was a buzz and whisper upon 'Change of a great failure. . . .
Next day it was noised abroad that Dombey and Son had
stopped, and next night there was a List of Bankrupts pub-
lished, headed by that name. . . . The strange faces of ac-
countants and others . . . quickly superseded all the old
clerks. . . . The Counting House soon got to be dirty and
neglected. . . . The swarm and buzz, and going up and down,
endure for days" (*Dombey and Son*, Chapters 58-59). Later
Florence Dombey kneels at Mr. Dombey's knees.

54(48). *Novaya zhizn'* [New life], no. 1 (January 1914). K2, K3,
K4. As an "inner exile," Mandelstam often identified with
his own biblical namesake, Joseph, as well as with Ovid.

55(50). K2, K3, K4. There is a fair copy with the title "Valkyr-
ies." Mandelstam echoes Pushkin's *Eugene Onegin* (l. 22.
3-12), which Vladimir Nabokov translates as

still the tired footmen
sleep on the pelisses at the carriage porch;
still people have not ceased to stamp,
blow noses, cough, hiss, clap;
still, outside and inside,
lanterns shine everywhere;
still, feeling chilled, the horses fidget,
bored with their harness,
and the coachmen around the fires
curse their masters and beat their palms together . . .

Mandelstam's description of *Die Walküre* (1870) as ponderous is endorsed by Robert W. Gutman in his *Richard Wagner* (New York: Harcourt Brace Jovanovich, 1968); he calls Act II "hippopotamic" (p. 169). The opera ends with the departure of the Valkyries on horses, after which Wotan puts Brünnhilde to sleep inside a ring of flames; the departing carriages and bonfires ironically recall this.

There was a Wagner cult among some of the Symbolist poets at this period.

56(261). K2. Manuscript has the title "Rome" and is dated 1914. See the lines from Tyutchev cited in the note to Poem 65. The dome is presumably that of St. Peter's, "completing" the Roman skyline and testifying to the triumph of Catholicism. The Aventine hill is associated with the plebians in Roman history; they gathered there during struggles with the patricians. There are now a number of churches and monasteries on the hill. The Twelve Feasts are the Twelve Great Feasts of the Orthodox Church: the Nativity of the Mother of God, the Exaltation of the Cross, the Presentation of the Mother of God in the Temple, the Nativity of Christ, the Baptism of Christ, the Presentation of Our Lord in the Temple, the Annunciation, the Entry of Our Lord into Jerusalem, the Ascension, Pentecost, the Transfiguration, the Falling Asleep of the Mother of God (Easter is not included, since it is in a superior and unique category). The Orthodox ecclesiastical year begins on 1 September; some of the feasts are movable and so depend on the solar rather than the ordinary calendar.

57(264). *Apollon*, no. 6-7 (August-September 1914). K2, K3, K4. The poem is titled "Before the War" in *Apollon*, has no title in K2, is titled "1913" in K3, and "Before the War" in K4. There is a fair copy dated 1914. Brown says that in 1937

Mandelstam cancelled this entire poem in a copy of K4 (B, p. 164). The Capitol, or Capitoline Hill, was the civic and religious center of ancient Rome. The word *peruny*, which Mandelstam uses for "thunderbolts" (l. 5), contains Peroun or Perun, the ancient Slavic god of thunder. Rome's "thunder" is the wrath of the Roman people, incited by Cicero or some other popular orator. The beaks are the bronze beaks (*rostra*) of ships captured at Antium (later replaced with those captured at Actium) that were affixed to the front of the orators' tribune (hence rostrum) in the Roman Forum. The premature child suggests Caesar, and the keys suggest the papacy. Mandelstam seems to be recollecting Tyutchev's "Napoleon's Tomb" ("Mogila Napoleona," 1828): "The *Peroun* [thundering] of his victories has been over for a long time,/And the rumble of them sounds all over the world"; he may also be recalling Tyutchev's "Cicero" ("Tsitseron," 1830): "The Roman orator spoke/Amid civic storms and alarms."

58(51). K4. A 1914 fair copy has two titles, "At my place on the Moon" and "Invitation to the Moon." The 1914 version, printed in SS as Poem 58b, is as follows:

> At my place on the moon
> There are waffles every day,
> Come to me
> My darling empress!
> No bread on the moon—
> Waffles every day.
>
> No grass grows on the moon,
> Not even a single blade;
> All the people on the moon
> Are in the basket-weaving trade—
> Light baskets woven
> Out of straw braid.
>
> Let's escape for an hour
> From the villain earth!
> There aren't any roads on the moon
> And benches are everywhere—
> When you step, it's a leap
> Across three benches!
>
> Take along with you
> Some milk for the kittens,

Wild strawberry jam from the woods,
An umbrella and comb . . .
I'll make you hot punch
On the blue moon.

Mandelstam came back to this poem in 1927, when he revised and expanded it (SS, poem 58a):

All that about the moon is only a tall tale,
It's not right to believe in that nonsense about the moon,
All that about the moon is only a tall tale . . .

[Then follow the two stanzas comprising 58]
There aren't any roads on the moon,
And benches are everywhere,
They water the sand
From a tall watering pot—
When you step, it's a leap
Across three benches.

At my place on the moon
There are blue fish,
But up there on the moon
They're not able to swim,
There's no water on the moon
And the fish fly . . .

59(52). *Giperborei*, no. 9-10. K2, K3, K4. The poem is dedicated to Anna Akhmatova in *Giperborei*, and it is titled "Akhmatova" in K2 and K3. Brown (p. 213) refers to an early draft that applies the epithet "poisoner" to Phèdre. I have followed K2, K3, and K4 in preferring the reading *dushi* to the SS reading *dusha* in line 6 (see B, p. 307, n. 1). According to Akhmatova's recollection, the poem was written at the beginning of January 1914; the issue of *Giperborei* in which it appeared was late and was not published until February 1914. She has also described the event that gave rise to the poem:

As for the poem "O sorrow—she half turned around,"
this is its history: in January 1914, Pronin threw a big
evening party for the "Stray Dog" crowd, not in the
"cave" but in some big hall on the Konyushennaya
[Street]. The regulars were lost in the crowd of
"strangers" (that is, strangers to any art). It was stuffy,
crowded, noisy, and rather pointless. After a while we

got tired of it so we (20-30 people) went to the "Dog" on Michael Square. It was cool and dark there. I was standing on the stage in conversation with somebody. Some people who had come from the hall began to ask me to recite some poems. Without altering my stance, I recited something. Osip came up: "The way you stood, the way you recited" [he said], and something about the shawl. (SS, 1: 420; see also AAS, 2: 172-173)

Boris Pronin, an actor, was the proprietor of "The Stray Dog." Rachel (1820-1858) was one of the greatest of French classical actresses, particularly celebrated for her performance of the title role in Racine's *Phèdre*. Mandelstam's lines evoke that play, especially Phèdre's first entrance (I, iii): ". . . these royal veils. They drag me to the ground. . . . I am crushed by ornaments./Everything hurts me and drags me to my knees." See Robert Lowell's translation in *The Classic Theatre*, ed. Eric Bentley (New York: Anchor Books, 1961), p. 4; and my note to Poem 81. Akhmatova's shawl is literally "pseudoclassical," but the term is less pejorative in Russian than in English. She often wore shawls and referred to them in her poems; Blok describes her in his "To Anna Akhmatova," written on 16 December 1913, a few weeks before Mandelstam's poem: "Languidly you toss/A Spanish shawl across your shoulders . . . "

60(53). *Golos zhizni* [The voice of life], no. 14 (1 April 1915). K2, K3, K4. In *Golos zhizni*, this poem appeared along with numbers 61 and 69 under the title "From the cycle 'Rome.'" In his diary (6 February 1915), Sergey Kablukov refers to the acceptance of these poems for publication by the editor of *Golos zhizni*, Zinaida Gippius, wife of Dmitry Merezhkovsky (BP). In *The Sound of Time*, Mandelstam says that "Clumsy doormen, bears with badges, dozed at their gates. That is how it was a quarter of a century ago" (P, p. 126). Brown (p. 309) suggests the poem's sources in Ovid's *Tristia*, the Roman poet's account of his exile to the coast of the Black Sea by Augustus for "a poem and a mistake" (*carmen et error*):

> et undas
> frigore concretas ungula pulsat equi;
> perque novos pontes, subter labentibus undis,
> ducunt Sarmatici barbara plaustra boves.
>
> (*Tristia* 3.10.31-34)

>   . . . and the waters,
> Made solid by the cold, feel the hoof beats of the horse.
> Over this newly made bridge, above the gliding currents,
> The oxen of the Sarmatians draw the barbarian carts.

The Scyths lived in southern Russia in classical times and are mentioned by many Greek and Roman writers. Gate-keepers, also called watchmen or yardmen, guarded large houses and opened the gates to visitors.

Mandelstam also evokes the figure of Ovid (Taranovsky, p. 45) as he is presented in Pushkin's *Tsigani* [The gypsies], where an old Gypsy tells of the poet's exile as if it were a recent event, and describes the kindness of the people:

> As the swift-running river froze
> And the winter storms raged,
> With a shaggy hide they covered
> The holy old man.

(Mandelstam quotes this Pushkin passage in "Concerning the Nature of the Word," SS, 2: 295.) Compare also stanza 1 of Verlaine's "Pensée du soir" (1887):

> Couché dans l'herbe pâle et froide de l'exil,
> Sous les ifs et les pins qu'argente le grésil,
> Ou bien errant, semblable aux formes que suscite
> Le rêve, par l'horreur du paysage scythe,
> Tandis qu'autour, pasteurs de troupeaux fabuleux,
> S'effarouchent les blancs Barbares aux yeux bleus,
> Le poète de l'art d'Aimer, le tendre Ovide
> Embrasse l'horizon d'un long regard avide
> Et contemple la mer immense tristement.

> An Evening Thought

> Couched on the pale cold grass of exile,
> Under the yews and pines which the snow makes silver,
> Or perhaps wandering, like forms evoked
> In a dream, through the horror of the Scythian landscape,
> While all around, shepherds of fabled flocks
> Are frightened by the white Barbarians with blue eyes,
> The gentle Ovid, the poet of the Art of Love,
> Scans the horizon with a long avid look
> And sadly contemplates the vast sea.

61(54). *Golos zhizni*, no. 14. K2, K3, K4. In *Golos zhizni*, this poem was titled "In Memory of Voronikhin" and appeared with numbers 60 and 69 under the general title "From the cycle 'Rome'." There and in K2, line 8 reads, "You walk through the grove of the portico," and line 12 is, "Pressed helplessly to the ground!" Sergey Kablukov's diary (6 September 1914) records an evening when Mandelstam read "From the cycle 'Rome' " along with poems 68, 63, 62, and 64 (BP). The poem was written in honor of the centenary of A. N. Voronikhin (1759-1814), a serf who was probably an illegitimate son of Count Stroganov. Voronikhin was the architect of the Kazan Cathedral in St. Petersburg, which contained the miraculous icon of the Virgin of Kazan; the building is now the Museum of Religion and Atheism. The cathedral is modeled on St. Peter's in Rome, with a dome and a semicircular colonnade of 136 Corinthian columns. The "gigantic rock" is St. Isaac's Cathedral (1819-1858), the largest church in St. Petersburg, designed by Ricard de Monferrand, apparently with a good deal of unsolicited advice from Nicholas I.

62(55). K2, K3, K4. A fair copy is titled "Midsummer," and Sergey Kablukov refers to it by this name in his diary (6 September 1914; see note to Poem 61). Taranovsky (pp. 143-144, n. 19) defends Mandelstam's use of "tonic" rather than "quantitative" to describe the meter of Greek poetry, which is determined by vowel length. Konstantin Mochulsky, who taught him some Greek in 1912, recalled his interest in sound rather than meaning: "The reading of Homer was transformed into a fabulous event; adverbs, enclitics, and pronouns hounded him in his sleep and he entered into enigmatic personal relationships with them. . . . He transformed grammar into poetry, and declared that the more incomprehensible Homer was, the more beautiful. . . . Mandelstam did not learn Greek, he intuited it" (B, p. 47; BP, pp. 264-265). Mochulsky quotes a two-stanza poem that Mandelstam wrote for him; one stanza reads as follows:

> And the bell of the verbal endings
> Shows the distant path I must
>   follow;
> In the sober philologist's cell
> I find relief from my sorrow.
>   (SS, poem 419)

Mandelstam may be recalling Tyutchev's "There is a melody in the waves of the sea" ("Pyevuchest' yest' v morskikh volnakh," 1865): "And a harmonious musical rustling/Runs through the tossing reeds." Tyutchev's poem has an epigraph from Ausonius, *Epistulae* (25.13): "Est in arundineis modulatio musica ripis" ("There is musical melody in the reeds along the bank"). See notes to poems 15 and 17.

63(56). *Novii Satirikon*, no. 26. K2, K3, K4. Titled "Ice Cream" in *Novii Satirikon*; Kablukov refers to it by that title in his diary (6 September 1914; see note to Poem 61). K2 prints line 5: "But to ask for a spoon; to gaze sweetly." Here the "tea room Graces" are among mountains, as are the Graces in Hesiod, where they dwell in a "festive house . . . Not far from the highest peak of snow clad Olympus" (*Theogony* 1. 63-68). Hesiod was among the Acmeist heroes; Mandelstam draws on the *Theogony* for poem 105, written in May 1919 (Taranovsky, p. 86).

64(262). K2, K3, K4. Kablukov's diary (6 September 1914) refers to this poem as "Ozerov the Tragedian" (see note to Poem 61). Alexander Sumarokov (1717-1777) wrote neoclassical tragedies and was known as "the Russian Racine." Vladislav Ozerov (1769-1816) was the last important writer of such tragedies. The "prophet's holy staff" is Aaron's rod, which Moses placed in the tabernacle as one of the twelve rods representing the Twelve Tribes: "the rod of Aaron for the house of Levi was budded, and brought forth buds, and bloomed blossoms, and yielded almonds" (Num. 17:8).

65(82). *Tristia*, 1922. K3, K4. Not dated in *Tristia*; BP asserts that this poem and Poem 66 were written in November 1917, on the evidence of a fair copy containing both poems. The text of this copy shows several variant readings:

> When Rome stood in union with nature,
> She wore the external forms of her civic power
> In the open air, like a blue circus,
> A forum of fields, or groves in a colonnade.
>
> But now there's a man—neither a slave nor a master—
> Not self-intoxicated, but only confused.
> We say involuntarily, "A citizen of the whole world,"
> But we want to say, "A villager of the whole world."

Compare Tyutchev, "Rome by Night" ("Rim noch'yu," 1850), which describes Rome by moonlight: "How Rome's eternal dust resembles [the moon's]! . . . /As if the lunar world and the sleeping city—/Were all one world, magical but dead! . . . " There is also an echo of Baudelaire's "Cor-

respondances": "Nature is a temple where living pillars"
[La Nature est un temple où de vivants piliers].

66(81). *Vechernyaya zvezda* [The evening star], 9 March 1918. K3, K4. Probably written in November 1917; see note to Poem 65.

67(57). K2, K3, K4. In 1762, James Macpherson (1736-1796) published *Fingal: An Ancient Epic Poem in Six Books*, which he claimed he had discovered and translated from the works of the third-century Scottish poet Ossian; in fact he had cobbled together some fragments of ancient Irish epic (Fingal is the Irish hero Finn) with some misty scenery to evoke a vaguely melancholy mood in cadences reminiscent of the King James Bible. These "poems of Ossian" were extremely popular and were translated into most European languages, including Russian (Ozerov wrote a tragedy called *Fingal*). Mandelstam is probably drawing on Tyutchev's "The Skald's Harp" ("Arfa skal'da"):

O harp of the skald! You have slept for a long time
In the shadow and dust of a forgotten corner;
But as soon as the moon, enchanting the dimness,
Shines its azure light into your corner,
Suddenly a beautiful chiming begins to reverberate in your
strings,
Like the delirium of a soul, startled in a dream.

What life did it breathe for you?
Did it recall ancient times for you . . .

(21 April 1834)

Gumilyov has a poem "Ossian" in his *Romanticheskie tsveti* [Romantic flowers, 1908], reworked from an earlier version, "A nocturnal and dark dream" ("Greza nuchnaya i temnaya") in his first book, *Put' konkvistadorov* [The path of the conquistadors, 1905].

68(58). *Apollon*, no. 6-7 (October 1914). K2, K3, K4. Manuscript dated September 1914. See note to Poem 61. In *Apollon*, stanza 3 reads:

> Europe of Augustus and the Sun King,
> But now in the rags of the Holy Alliance,
> The heel of Spain and the gentle medusa,
> The land of Italy, the Roman land.

In *The Egyptian Stamp*, Parnok likes to look at a map and compare "the airy outlines of Aryan Europe with the blunt boot of Africa" (P, p. 153). Prince Metternich, Austrian minister of foreign affairs from 1809 to 1848, negotiated the various treaties that fixed the boundaries of most European nations after the downfall of Napoleon; most of these boundaries were not altered until World War I. He also assisted in forming the Holy Alliance of Austria, Russia, and Prussia to oppose and suppress any revolutionary or democratic movements in Europe. From 1815 to 1918, Poland was officially a kingdom, but it was ruled by the Russian emperor through a viceroy.

69(59). *Golos zhizni*, no. 14. K2, K3, K4. In *Golos zhizni*, this poem appeared with poems 60 and 61 under the general title, "From the cycle 'Rome' " and with the following variants: "I took staff in hand and rejoiced" (l.7); "To me, marching on Rome" (l. 16); and, as stanza 3:

> I know the snow on the black fields
> Will never melt away,
> Nor does the water from domestic vineyards
> Every intoxicate me.

Gleb Struve has demonstrated that this poem is about the Russian philosopher Pyotr Chaadaev (1793?-1856), who was for Mandelstam a forerunner on the journey to Rome and the classical heritage of the West. See Gleb Struve, "Italian Images and Motifs in the Poetry of Osip Mandelstam" ("Ital'ianskie obrazy i motivy v poezii Osipa Mandel'štama"), in *Studi in onore di Ettore Lo Gatto e Giovanni Maver* (Roma: Sansoni Editore, 1962). (The title has been cited in English as a courtesy to the reader: no English translation exists.) In a 1914 essay on Chaadaev, which appeared in *Apollon*, no. 6-7 Mandelstam wrote: "Russia gave Chaadaev only one gift: moral freedom, freedom of choice. No one in the West had gained this freedom in such magnitude, in such purity and plenitude. Chaadaev accepted it as a sacred staff and walked to Rome" (SS, 2: 333). Chaadaev believed that Russia was tragically cut off from the civilization of Western Europe and that Catholicism, embodied in the papacy, shaped and preserved that civilization. His *Lettres philosophiques*, written in French and begun about 1830, declared that Russian Christianity was tainted because it came from a tainted source, Byzantium; that Russia had passed from barbarism (the Kievan period) to a foreign (Mongol) domination whose forms still per-

241

sisted under the Tsars: and that all Russians were nomads in their own country. He urges a greater acceptance of Western ideas and culture and praises the civilizing and moral force of the papacy. When the first letter was published (1836), Chaadaev was certified as insane, a Russian method of dealing with political dissidents that has been revived in our own time. Mandelstam seems to connect Chaadaev's staff with Aaron's rod in poems 64 and 72.

70(77). *Vechernyaya zvezda*, 16 February 1918. *Tristia*, 1922. K3, K4. Dated 1916 in *Vechernyaya zvezda* and *Tristia*; there is a fair copy dated 1916 and a rough draft on the same sheet as SS, poem 86 ("Solominka"), written in December 1916. This contains a variant for stanza 3:

> O Europe, O new land of Hellas,
> Golden granary for guests,
> We need neither the love nor the friendship
> Of Albion's stone children.

There is also a discarded stanza 4:

> In the sacred memory of the people
> The English did not have a reputation for friendship,
> Their liberty will destroy Europe,
> Albion's stony arrival.

BP quotes Sergey Kablukov's diary (2 January 1917): "He [Mandelstam] was showing dislike . . . for the English, who he considers arrogant, self-satisfied, and Philistine—a self-satisfied insular nation alien in spirit and opposed to the continent."

The Salamis reference is not to the Athenian victory over the Persians but to an exploit of Solon as recorded by Plutarch. Having failed to capture the island of Salamis from the Megarians, the Athenians passed a law forbidding anyone to advocate another expedition. Solon pretended to be insane, and then publicly recited some verses that he had written, beginning

> I come as a herald from charming Salamis
> To tell you in a poem rather than a speech
> What should be done.

His auditors were stirred to action, and Solon led them to the conquest of the island (Plutarch *Solon* 8). See Terras, p. 258. Terras assumes that the poem was written in 1914, but Mandelstam seems to be referring to events in Greece in late 1916: Britain and France tried to persuade the Greek government to join the Allies and, when the Greeks refused, demanded the surrender of the Greek fleet (10 October 1916). On 30 November, French and British forces landed at Piraeus, the port of Athens. They withdrew the next day, only to blockade Greece on 8 December, and a little later to impose a new government on Greece.

71(266). *Nevskii al'manakh* [Nevsky almanac], 1915. K2. There is a fair copy with the title "On the Encyclical of Pope Benedict XV" dated September 1914; in *Nevskii al'manakh* and K2, the title was simply "Encyclica" (K2: "Encyclyca"). World War I began when various nations declared war between 28 July and 6 August 1914. Pope Pius X (1903-1914) issued an appeal for peace on 2 August and died on 20 August; Benedict XV was elected on 3 September but did not issue his first encyclical (a formal letter in which the Pope addresses the hierarchy of the entire Church or of a single country, and through them the faithful) until November. Mandelstam may have mistakenly attributed Pius's last appeals for peace to Benedict, or he may be thinking of some plea for peace from the new Pope less formal than an encyclical. The view of the papacy here is close to Chaadaev's, who is "the man/Who spoke to me of Rome" in lines 11-12 (see the article by G. P. Struve cited in the note to Poem 69). Mandelstam is, in a sense, replying to Tyutchev's strongly antipapal "Encyclica" (21 December 1864), an attack on Pius IX for his encyclical *Quanta cura* (8 December 1864) and its attached "Syllabus of Errors," which claimed that the Church ought to control all cultural, scientific, and educational activities, and explicitly denied man's right to freedom of conscience and worship. Tyutchev recalls how "the hammer of the Lord of truth" once destroyed the Temple in Jerusalem and killed the High Priest:

> Yet more terribly, yet more inexorably—
> In our own days—the days of God's judgment—
> An execution will be carried out in apostate Rome
> Upon the false vicar of Christ.
>
> In the centuries gone by he has been forgiven much,
> Twisted doctrine and murky deeds,
> But the God of truth will not forgive
> His most recent crime . . .

243

The thunder in lines 5 and 6 of Poem 71 suggests the sonorous Latin of Papal pronouncements, the "guns of August" against which the Pope speaks, and the Old Testament God's habit of speaking in thunder: "God thundereth marvellously with his voice; great things doth he, which we cannot comprehend" (Job 37:4-5).

72(60). *Al'manakhi stikhov*, Vol. 1, *Tsevnitsa*. K2, K3, K4. The poem was complete in the *Al'manakhi stikhov* and K2; Mandelstam later deleted the bracketed lines and replaced them with dots indicating the deletion. The manuscript is dated 6 December 1914 and contains a different version of lines 29-32:

> Sensing you in the darkness,
> Chenier accepted his fate with dignity,
> When he shone like a demigod
> Upon the black tumbril.

Beethoven is a "Flemish peasant's son" (1. 21) because his father came from Antwerp. A *ritornelle* (1. 23) or *ritornello* is an instrumental refrain in a vocal work; Mandelstam seems to imagine it as the music for a dance, presumably with repetition both of refrain and dance figure. The shrine and tent are those used by the Israelites in the wilderness, as described in Exodus 25-27. St. Paul (Acts 17:23) discovered an altar in Athens inscribed "To the Unknown God" (1. 40).

BP points out that line 42 quotes Tyutchev's "A Last Love" ("Poslednyaya lyubov," ca. 1853): "The shadow spread over half the sky" (1. 5).

The "Ode" is related to Mandelstam's essay "Pushkin and Scriabin" (SS, 2: 355-361; see B, pp. 230-235), probably begun about 1915 and completed in 1919-1920; it was not published during Mandelstam's lifetime and exists only in fragments. The essay contrasts Pushkin and the composer Alexandr Scriabin (1871-1915), but its fragmentary state makes the argument difficult to follow. Mandelstam disapproves of Scriabin's shift away from Christianity toward theosophy, and in his essay implicitly attacks the mystical Symbolists: The essay praises the "wholeness" of Christian art and Christian music. Mandelstam addresses Beethoven as "Dionysus" (1. 25) because the essay describes Dionysus as the "destructive element" that the ancient Greeks feared in "pure music," that is, music unaccompanied by words. Christianity was not afraid of this "destructive element" and allowed pure music, challenging Dionysus and channeling the energy he represents. Mandelstam imagines Christianity addressing Dionysus: " 'Well then, try it, command that I be torn to pieces by your maenads. I am all wholeness, all that is personal, all cohesive unity!' . . . This certainty about personal salvation . . . comes as an overtone into Christian music, turning the sonority of Beethoven into the white marble of Sinaic glory" (SS, 2: 358). Mandelstam is presumably thinking of Michelangelo's statue of a majestically angry Moses with the tablets of the law, originally designed for the tomb of Pope Julius II—hence the reference to the tent that enclosed the Ark of the Covenant; tent and Ark were constructed according to God's specifications as given to Moses on Mount Sinai. Mandelstam quotes the last line of the "Ode" in the essay: "The catholic joy of Beethoven, the synthesis of the Ninth Symphony, that 'triumph of a radiating glory,' is not accessible to Scriabin" (SS, 2: 359).

Mandelstam's description of Beethoven walking in a storm reproduces passages found in biographies of the composer, and it reminds us that he is a real man, not a demigod. Beethoven is not afraid of thunder because he too "thunders" (like the Pope in Poem 71) and draws down fire from heaven; the burning pages of lines 7-8 are consumed in the fire of creativity, or perhaps "burn" as the music is performed. The poem's general preoccupation with fire and lightning suggests some of Beethoven's musical effects, and Mandelstam is probably also thinking of Scriabin's Fourth Symphony, the "Prometheus," also known as the "Poem of Fire." In *The Sound of Time*, Mandelstam mentions "the silk flame of the Nobility Hall and frail Scriabin, whom one expected to see crushed at any moment by the still mute semicircle of singers about him and the string forest of *Prometheus*" (P, p. 94).

73(61). *Rudin*, no. 8 (April-May 1916); *Krasnaya nov'* [Red virgin soil], no. 4 (July-August 1922). K3, K4. The manuscript is dated 1915 and adds two more stanzas at the end:

> Tell the desert
> About the wood of the cross;

Such loveliness
In the heart's deep core!

I made a boat
Out of plain wood,
And I could not imagine
Anything else to make.

74(63). *Novii Satirikon*, no. 42 (1916). K2, K3, K4. The poem is
dated 1915 in K2 and 1914 in K4. In *Novii Satirikon*, there
is a fourth stanza:

Everything on earth has changed
Except this, that the land has not cast off
The soutane cut in the Roman pattern
And your gold, o fields.
And our most modest contemporary,
Jammes, sings like a lark—
After all, a Catholic priest
Gives him advice!

Francis Jammes (1868-1938), a French Catholic poet, wrote
of peasants and their simple piety in such works as *Géor-
giques chrétiennes*, 1912. A manuscript contains the above
stanza as stanza 1, followed by

The priest hears the song of a bird
And any fresh news;
All his glory is fed
By the radiance of his tonsured nimbus.
A wonderful light shines from it
When he walks in the evening
Or when he strolls on the market square in the morning
And gives alms to those who beg.

And when we met I bowed to him, and he
Responded with a civil nod of the head,
And then, as he chatted there with me,
"You will die a Catholic," he said.
It is like a diamond cutting
Through the thickness of despondency and idleness
When we remember the new home
That awaits us in Rome!

There a canonical happiness
Stands at the zenith, like the sun,
And no autocracy
Will forbid it to shine.

O lark, o nimble captive,
Who will better capture your song
Than a Catholic priest
In July, in a harvest year!

The abbé is tonsured, that is, he has a shaved or bare spot about the size of a half-dollar at the crown of his head in accordance with canon law as then observed in France and other continental countries; this spot is first shaved as part of the preparations for ordination, but in later life shaving is often not necessary. Clarence Brown asked Akhmatova if this poem was based on any real incident. She replied that it was "pure literature" (B, p. 197).

75(62). K2, K4. Written in June 1915. The *Imyabozhtsi* or "God's Name" movement began about 1910 in the Russian monastery on Mount Athos. It taught that God's name is itself divine. Man cannot approach God directly nor glorify Him directly, but can only approach and glorify His name. The Synod of the Russian Church declared this doctrine heretical in 1915, after it had spread to many Russian monasteries and had attracted interest among intellectuals.

76(64). K3, K4. Written early in 1915.

77(65). K2, K3, K4. Written in June 1915.

78(66). K2, K3, K4. Written in the summer of 1915, when Mandelstam was staying in the Crimea. The "catalogue of ships" in the *Iliad* lists the leaders of the expedition against Troy, the city from which each came, and the number of ships accompanying them (2. 484-877). Shortly before the catalogue begins, there is a muster of the Achaean host:

These, as the multitudinous nations of birds winged,
of geese, and of cranes, and of swans long-throated
in the Asian meadow beside the Kaÿstrian waters
this way and that way make their flights in the pride of
    their wings, then
settle in clashing swarms and the whole meadow echoes
    with them,
so of these the multitudinous tribes from the ships and
shelters poured to the plain of Skamandros, and the earth
    beneath their
feet and under the feet of the horses thundered horribly.
                            (*Iliad* 2. 459-466;
                            trans. Richmond Lattimore.
                            See Terras, p. 258.)

In his "Talking about Dante" ("Razgovor o Dante"), Mandelstam comments:

> Dante's similes are never descriptive, that is, purely
> representational. They always pursue the concrete goal
> of giving the inner image of the structure or the force.
> Let us take the very large group of bird similes—all
> those long caravans now of cranes, now of crows, and
> now the classical military phalanxes of swallows, now
> the anarchically disorderly ravens, unsuited to Latin
> military formations—this group of extended similes al-
> ways corresponds to the instinct of pilgrimage, travel,
> colonization, migration. (Dante, p. 77. See also Monas,
> p. 15; SS, 2: 416)

The cranes work simultaneously as a simile for the ships
(which were also "hatched" or given birth to by Hellas), as
a metaphor for both the literal journey of the Achaeans and
the poet's imaginative journey, as a quotation of one of Ho-
mer's similes (used several times in his work), and as a met-
aphor for poetry's ability to take form in letters and to cross
national and linguistic boundaries (see the development of
this theme in Poem 67). According to legend, Hermes
formed the letters of the Greek alphabet by imitating the
wedge formation in which cranes fly. In "Talking about
Dante," Mandelstam reminds us that Dante's pen was a
bird's feather: "Dante, who never forgets the origin of
things, remembers this. His technique of writing in broad
strokes and curves grows into the figured flight of flocks of
birds." (Dante, p. 10. See also Monas, p. 40; SS, 2: 416.)

Taranovsky (p. 147, n. 6) connects this poem with Poem
18 because of its water imagery and its motif of falling
asleep. He emphasizes its dependence on Gnedich's Rus-
sian version of the *Iliad* (1829). Nils Åke Nilsson ("Osip
Mandel'štam's 'Insomnia' Poem," *International Journal of
Slavic Linguistics and Poetics* 10 [1966]: 148-154) provides
a general discussion of the poem and relates it to a tradition
of "insomnia" poems, citing Pushkin's "Verses Written at
Night in a Time of Sleeplessness" ("Stikhi sochinnenniye
noch'yu vo vremiya bessonitsi," 1830) and Innokenty An-
nensky's cycle "Insomnia" ("Bessonnitsi," 1904). In collec-
tions of Pushkin's work, his "Sleeplessness" verses are usu-
ally followed, within a page or two, by his epigram on
Gnedich's *Iliad*.

79(268). K3. The manuscript is dated August 1915, when Mandelstam was in Feodosia, in the Crimea, and contains variant texts for stanzas 1 and 4:

> Offended, the plebians move off among the knolls,
> Sheep filled with longing for a seven-hilled Rome,
> They wander the black waves of the land
> In an ocean of darkness.

This is followed by stanzas 3 and 4 of the printed version, which are in reverse order in the manuscript; then comes a final stanza:

> They are enthralled by acute blindness,
> They are the fleece of tongue-tied night;
> There is no sun upon them: their rheumy eyes
> Shine in the darkness like a prophet's vision.

Chaldaeans are a Semitic people, originally from the head of the Persian Gulf; their history is bound up with that of Assyria and Babylon. They were learned in magic and divination, so much so that in Latin the word *Chaldaeus* is synonymous with magician, wizard, or astrologer. Rome's Aventine hill is particularly associated with the plebians, who often assembled there during political confrontations with the patricians (Terras, p. 256). These Roman references suggest that a Roman is speaking, presumably the exiled Ovid (see poems 60 and 80); like Ovid, Mandelstam is writing on the shores of the Black Sea, and this poem is closely connected with Poem 80.

Ovid uses black wool or fleece as a metaphor for his own ill-fortune: "hic quoque cognosco natalis stamina nostri,/ stamina de nigro vellere facta mihi" [I recognize here too the threads of my destiny since birth, threads woven for me from a black fleece; *Tristia* 4. 1. 63-64]. This passage occurs just before a description of the perpetual state of siege in which the people of Tomi—Ovid's place of exile, Constanta in modern Roumania—habitually lived (ll. 65-86). Ovid equates some frightened sheep (frightened at once by both wolves and barbarians) with their frightened owners. The bushes that seem like the walls of a sheepfold echo Ovid's reference to sheepfolds (*ovili*, l. 79), while a later passage about the tensions of frontier life explains the warriors' tents or shelters: in Tomi, "sub galea pastor iunctis pice cantat avenis,/proque lupo pavidae bella verentur oves" [the shepherd plays his pipes that are fastened with pitch while wearing a helmet, and the terrified ewes fear war rather than the wolf; *Tristia* 5. 10. 25-26). Ovid stresses the incongruity of this state of affairs, when a piping shepherd must wear a warrior's helmet. Since these shepherds are also warriors, Mandelstam's frightened sheep imagine that the tents in their path are rushing at them, and he calls them warriors' tents rather than the expected shepherds' tents.

80(67). K2, K3, K4. Written at Feodosia in August 1915. The speaker is again Ovid (Terras, pp. 256-257). Caesar is Augustus, who ordered Ovid into exile. Steven Broyde explains "sovereign apple" in his *Osip Mandel'štam and His Age* (Cambridge: Harvard University Press, 1975) by citing on page 191 F. A. Brokgauz (Brockhaus) and I. A. Efron, *Ènciklopedičeskij slovar'* (St. Petersburg, 1899), 26: 445:

> The *orb* having the form of a [gold] globe . . . is a symbol of dominion over the land. Globes having this meaning are found on Roman coins of the emperor Augustus. . . . The orb came to Russia from Poland where it was called apple and in olden times it carried the name *apple of the czar's rank, apple of command,* and simply *apple.*

BP cites Pushkin's poem "On the hillocks of Georgia a nocturnal haze lies" ("Na kholmakh Gruzii lezhit nochnaya mgla," 1829) in connection with line 13; Brown cites line 2 of the same poem, "I am sorrowful and easy; my sadness is luminous" (B, pp. 194-195). The she-wolf (l. 15) recalls the Roman legend of Romulus and Remus. See also the passage from Verlaine's "Pensée du soir" cited in the note to Poem 60. These two Ovidian poems provide a kind of preparation for Mandelstam's poem "Tristia" (SS, poem 104) and also for the collection *Tristia.*

81(68). K2, K3, K4. Reciting this poem, Mandelstam once substituted *glory (slava)* for *faint (slabo)* in line 20: "And glory smells of orange peel" instead of "And there is a faint odor of orange peel." Gumilyov was delighted at the change, urged Mandelstam to retain it, and when the poet read the poem publicly he did say *glory* (SS).

Line 9, "These veils . . . ," partly translates Racine's *Phèdre* I. iii. 6: "How these useless ornaments, how these veils weigh me down" ("que ces vains ornaments, que ces voiles me pèsent"), and recalls, with line 14, Mandelstam's comparison of Akhmatova and Rachel in Poem 59. The curtain of line 10 suggests a sentence of Gumilyov's in his "The Legacy of Symbolism and Acmeism" ("Nasledie simvolizma i akmeizm"): "Here [i.e. in this life] death is the curtain separating us, the actors, from the spectators" (Gumilyov, 4: 174). Robert Lowell, who translated *Phèdre*, paraphrased Mandelstam's lines 10 and 11 in his comment upon the play: "Behind each line is a, for us, lost knowledge of actors and actresses, the stage and the moment" (see his note in Bentley, ed., *The Classic Theatre*, p. 472). In K3, Mandelstam followed this poem with a translation of part of the first scene of *Phèdre* (SS, poem 460), which he presumably intended as a kind of bridge to the first poem in *Tristia* (SS, poem 82), which is spoken by Phaedra and begins with the same line of Racine cited above: "How oppressive is the splendor of these veils and this attire amid my shame!" (see B, pp. 207-215). Melpomene (l. 23) is the Muse of Tragedy.

LIBRARY OF CONGRESS CATALOGING IN PUBLICATION DATA

Mandel'shtam, Osip Émil'evich, 1891-1938.
  Osip Mandelstam's Stone.

  (The Lockert library of poetry in translation)
  Includes bibliographical references.
  1. Tracy, Robert, 1928-   II. Title.
PG3476.M355K313   1981   891.71'3   80-7545
ISBN 0-691-06444-X
ISBN 0-691-01376-4 (pbk.)